From

The Women's Press Ltd
124 Shoreditch High Street, London E1

Angela Coyle *Photo by Roy Peters*

Angela Coyle is a sociology researcher at the University of Aston in Birmingham. Her work is especially focussed on aspects of women's employment. She is a feminist and a mother, and lives in Birmingham.

ANGELA COYLE

Redundant Women

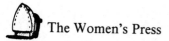
The Women's Press

First published by The Women's Press Ltd 1984
A member of the Namara Group
124 Shoreditch High Street, London E1 6JE

British Library Cataloguing in Publication Data

Coyle Angela
    Redundant women. – (The Women's Press handbook series)
    1. Employees, Dismissal of – Great Britain
    2. Women – Employment – Great Britain
    1. Title
    306'36   HF5549.5.D.55

    ISBN 0–7043–3923–4

Photoset by A.K.M. Associates (U.K.) Ltd, Southall, London
Printed in Great Britain by Nene Litho
and bound by Woolnough Bookbinding
both of Wellingborough, Northants

Contents

Acknowledgments

The research for this study was funded by the Equal Opportunities Commission and I am indebted to them for enabling this book to get written. Many, many people have helped me along the way. My thanks are due to Christine Jackson, Ron Barrowclough and Sue Speakman of the EOC for their encouragement and support; to the erstwhile Department of Sociology and Social History at the University of Aston in Birmingham, and particularly to Colin Bell, for providing an institutional home for the research; to Sue and Andy Winterburn and Mary and Chris Eusden for providing me with very much more than accommodation during the period of fieldwork; to Janice Winship, Angela Lloyd and Tony Elger for reading drafts of the manuscript; to Anne Lane for transforming scribbles into a typescript, and to Robert, Katherine and Daniel Coyle and Marina Vitale for domestic calm during the writing frenzy. My greatest debt is to the women and men who gave me so much of their time and who have provided the substance of this book.

Introduction

Twenty years ago, having spent half her life as a full-time housewife and mother of three children, my mother made a bid for freedom. She went out and got herself a job. She worked as a sales assistant in a local store. The work was hard and tiring, she got paid a pittance and it caused untold domestic ructions, yet for better or for worse, it depends where you stand, things were never the same again. She was never again my father's dependant. This private, domestic revolution was part of a wider social and economic trend in post-war Britain – the growth of women's employment outside of the home. Of course women's paid employment has not been confined to the post-war period. Women made up an important labour reserve in the early period of British industrialisation (until the nineteenth-century Factory Acts both protected and *confined* women's employment) and in both World Wars. Nevertheless, the perceptible trend for the first half of the twentieth century had been the steady decline in employment for *married* women; from 25 percent in 1851 to 13 percent in 1900 and 12 percent in 1921. From 1948 however, this downward trend has been reversed. Economic expansion in Britain from the 1950s onwards created more and more jobs for women. There has been a very long-term trend of growth of the female labour force, and, most significantly, that increase is largely attributable to the increase of *married* women at work. So that, by 1977, 50.4 percent of married women were economically active[1] (Department of Employment/DOE, 1981), which represented two-thirds of the total female labour force (Equal Opportunities Commission/EOC, 1979, p. 38).

1

The movement of women into employment has not been evenly distributed and women predominate in certain jobs and certain industries. In part the unevenness reflects the pattern of economic expansion; the growth of the service sector and the relative decline of manufacturing. It has been the expansion of the service sector in the post-war period which has provided the significant increase in the number of jobs available for women. It is an expansion which is considered to be integral to the dynamic of capitalist development (Baran and Sweezey, 1973; Braverman, 1974; Mandel, 1978). It represents an extension of the social division of labour and a capitalisation of many of the functions and services previously provided by the family. It was made possible by accelerated economic growth and the creation of capital surplus, which occurred in Britain through the periods 1940–1945 and 1945–1966 (Mandel, 1978). This growth began in the context of post-war restructuring; expansionist Keynesian policies of full employment, state intervention and the establishment of the Welfare State. It has occurred both in private services (finance, marketing, advertising, distribution, banking and retailing) and in the public sector (health, education and social services). That this growth would lead to more employment for women was 'neither accidental, nor unforeseen' (Counter Information Services/CIS, 1976) and incorporated into the Labour Party's National Plan for 1965. By 1971, Britain had made the shift to a 'service economy' with two-thirds of all women employees concentrated in that sector. Three industries: distributive trades, professional and scientific services and miscellaneous services, accounted for one-half of all women's jobs (DOE, 1974).

The service sector is especially labour intensive, and indeed Braverman has argued its expansion *premised* on the availability of cheap labour, female labour (1974, pp. 395–6). Services were not the first to 'discover' the specific cheapness of women's labour. In the inter-war period, women were increasingly employed on certain jobs in manufacturing, on labour-intensive, unskilled work, which was difficult or expensive to mechanise. Then, as now, women in manufacturing were employed in only four industries; food and drink manufacture, clothing and footwear,

2

textiles and electrical engineering. Now, as then, the same rule of thumb locates women's work in those industries. On the whole women have been confined to low-paid, unskilled work, and in a narrow range of occupations and industries. Women's relative access to skilled jobs, better-paid jobs and jobs of responsibility, has actually deteriorated (Hakim, 1979). What is clear is that women, and married women in particular, have been drawn into the labour force to provide a cheap, flexible source of labour, and are employed in what is effectively a female ghetto. There have now been various explanations of this utilisation of female labour (see, for example, Barrett, 1980; Beechey, 1978; Bland *et al.*, 1978). Work for women outside of the home has developed not instead of but in addition to unpaid domestic labour in the home. Women have acquired a 'dual role', in which they *combine* paid work with the unpaid domestic work of the family. This modification, rather than transformation, of the sexual division of labour between men and women is the crux of the matter. The subordination of women in the family allows for a specific exploitation of women at work. Consequently, the emancipating effect of employment for women is contradictory, and limited. Rather than clearly eroding gender divisions, employers exploit and develop them to great effect.

Nevertheless, the other side of that contradiction is that the transformation of women's lives through their paid work has been staggering. Women have formal equality with men, some financial independence, and domesticity is no longer expected to be the sole, life-long occupation of women. Work for women has been a route out of the domestic arena. Without this work it is hard to imagine that the transformation in women's lives during the post-war period could have taken place. What was once a domestic battle has become for me, my mother's daughter, and a post-war generation of women, normal circumstance.

Rising levels of unemployment in recession, now threaten the gains made by women in the post-war period. Since the early 1970s the level of unemployment in the UK has been rising, and from 1979 onwards has rocketed to levels that are now well over three million.[2] Officially women make up a little less than one-third of

3

the registered unemployed, but the *rate* at which women are becoming unemployed is twice as fast as it is for men, and there is evidence that nearly one-half of unemployed women are not registered as such. It could be that women's unemployment is now double the official figures.

The loss of women's jobs is occurring in part through the impact of recession and the contraction of the markets, but in recession, industries and services, both private and public, are reorganising methods of work and introducing labour-saving technology to increase productivity. A process of restructuring and reorganisation of the economy is taking place which is rationalising *labour-intensive work*, that is, the kind of work in which most women are employed. Such changes will cause *permanent* job loss rather than temporary contraction in recession. This restructuring initially affected men's jobs, but now women are disproportionately vulnerable because, unlike men, they are concentrated so heavily in a narrow range of jobs and industries. The long-term trends are difficult to envisage. The extent to which women will have access to jobs *created* by restructuring and new technology remains unclear. There is no evidence that women's opportunities for training or new occupations has widened at all.

So what does unemployment for women now mean? Does it mean a reversal of post-war changes? There has not only been a remarkable lack of government concern over rising female unemployment but, more ominously, women are losing their jobs in a climate unsympathetic to women's employment, let alone unemployment. For example, in September 1982, changes in the National Insurance regulations which were introduced as cost-saving measures, had the effect of making it *more difficult* for women to register as unemployed. When this is combined with the revival of old and familiar pearls of wisdom which oppose women working, women indeed seem in jeopardy.

In financial terms alone, unemployment amongst women must have some effect. Apart from an ever increasing number of women who are the sole 'breadwinners' for their families – 725,000 women in 1978, representing a 45 percent increase since 1971 (EOC, 1981b, p. 78) – it is increasingly clear that the male wage alone does not provide an adequate standard of living for the majority of families. It is a wife's wage that 'lifts' the family out of poverty (Royal Commission on the Distribution of Income and Wealth, 1978). Not only is women's employment an economic necessity, women express it to be an integral part of their lives and essential for them to attain a sense of themselves (Wood, 1981). Far from being the casual labour force that they are represented to be, women are as stable in their employment as their jobs will allow. Interruptions in employment amongst women are far more likely to occur through the unstable nature of women's employment, rather than through the personal characteristics or domestic circumstances of women (Elias and Main, 1982, p. 36). In fact, given the overwhelming concentration of women in the less stable sectors of the economy (Barron and Norris, 1976; Rubery, 1978), it is quite remarkable that women have in fact the same rate of job mobility as men in comparable age groups (Central Statistical Office/CSO, 1981, p. 78). Given the importance of women's employment, unemployment must be having a significant, rather than a negligible impact, yet there is no protest. The aim of this research was to investigate that quiescence.

In December 1980, a clothing manufacturer closed down two of its factory sites in Yorkshire, one in Harrogate and one in Castleford, and made nearly 300 people redundant. This book is an account of an experience of redundancy and draws largely upon taped conversations that I had with 30 women and 14 men from the Harrogate factory, and 29 women from the Castleford factory, as well as interviews with local management and trade union representatives. The small number of men employed at the Harrogate factory offered a limited, but valuable, basis for comparison between men and women. However the weight of the study focused on the women whom I interviewed at length, in their homes, over the period from October 1981 to June 1982. It offered the opportunity to determine the impact of unemployment on women, in the context of the conditions of the local labour market, and in the context of their domestic, familial circumstances. The time lapse from the redundancy to the first interviews did mean that the immediate impact of job loss could only be reported and understood with hindsight, but the gain was a much longer perspective of a labour market situation arising from a period of unemployment.

Chapters 1 to 3 tell the story of a redundancy. There are accounts of the clothing industry itself and how structural changes are causing job loss; of one firm's strategy for survival in recession, which included a massive cutback in manufacturing interests; of the impact of closure on a predominantly female labour force, their responses to job loss and their subsequent 'fate' on the labour market. Chapter 4 provides five women's more personalised versions of that experience, and Chapters 5, 6 and 7 reflect on the problems facing women in unemployment *and* employment. In the 1980s unemployment is one aspect of a worsening employment situation for women. The core of this book has ended up not just investigating women's unemployment, but considering the very nature of women's working lives. Although women are increasingly sharing with men the responsibility of wage earning, there is no indication that men are significantly sharing the responsibility of domestic work with women. Women still have to combine their paid employment with the unpaid work of the household. Yet this dual role of women is not fixed forever and at different points in a woman's life cycle, the domestic and paid employment variously assume different degrees of importance. The period of a woman's life which is most dominated by the family is a short one and, as it diminishes, work provides women with a wage which purchases economic independence within the family, and with a set of social relationships outside of the family, from which women derive a crucial sense of themselves. If women's paid work appears 'overdetermined' by the domestic routine, could it be that men, as bosses, workers and husbands, have an interest in keeping them there?

1
The Clothing Trade

Clothing is a woman's industry in that it employs a larger proportion of women than any other (80 percent). Since the war, it has suffered from increasing foreign competition and has been in slow decline, shedding approximately 2 percent of its labour force every year. In recession, long-term decline has rapidly accelerated and job loss is now occurring at a rate of 12 percent per annum. Competition has intensified and strategies to try and cope with this, and to increase productivity, have themselves contributed to further job loss. The problems facing clothing are similar to other labour-intensive industries, but are more acute because its existence has been premised largely on the exploitation of female labour. It has been possible to pay *very* low wages indeed and therefore to be profitable on the basis of very small capital outlay. In the long term, this low capital composition of the industry has been the underlying cause of its low productivity and economic decline. Recession has forced greater capital investment, but as long as it remains possible to pay low wages to women it will remain a disincentive towards further investment. The very ethics of clothing are that women are there to sweat.

Pay and Conditions

The industry is made up of an extraordinarily wide range of producers with diverse products and production methods. A clothing factory can be a large-scale enterprise employing a labour force of over a thousand and utilising the most advanced technology available, or it can be a small sweatshop, employing a handful of women working on very basic sewing machines. What unites the industry is the low wages paid to its predominantly female labour force. Where factories are unionised, pay is usually based on nationally-agreed rates negotiated by the National Union of Tailors and Garment Workers (NUTGW) and the Clothing Employers' Federation. There are, additionally, some local agreements and, of course, many non-unionised workplaces where wage rates vary with individual employers. Wage Council regulations set the minimum rates of pay for the industry as a whole, that is, the lowest rate that can be legally paid. Minimum rates often become the going rate, and even in unionised factories the Wage Council minimum provides the basis for negotiations (Roche, 1970, p. 162). The extent to which wages earned exceed the minimum rate will vary according to how far the union is able to negotiate a better rate – and the union is not strong – and how hard women work. Clothing employers favour a payment system which combines a particularly low basic rate with a productivity bonus. Any woman who comes out at the end of the week with a good wage, will have earned every penny of it: 'Well to bring that money home you had to work like heck for it and sometimes you didn't dare even to go to the toilet because every single minute counted, and I'm a bit dodgy on my nerves and I used to get all het up, to try and keep my numbers going to keep my wages up.'

Low rates of pay are only part of the problem. The method of payment is the other. Piece work of one form or another has been a common payment system in the clothing industry. Since the 1970s, 'science' in the form of time and motion study has been applied to piece work with a vengeance, and the NUTGW have found themselves negotiating agreements which they do not fully understand (*Garment Worker*, March 1973; Roche, 1970). The most common payment system in the industry is now a payment by results scheme which sets a 'standard performance' for each operation, known in the trade as 'the standard 100 performance'.[3] This is defined as: 'The rate of output which qualified workers will naturally achieve without over-exertion as an average over the working day or shift, provided they know and adhere to the specific method and provided they are motivated to apply themselves to their work' (quoted in Roche, 1970, p. 163).

This work study devises methods of work by which a garment can be assembled in the fastest possible time. This involves breaking down the assembly process into a sequence of simple operations, with a 'specific method' established for each operation. Then it can be performed at high speed, over and over again, by a semi-skilled operative trained in only one or two such operations. Skilled workers are bitterly opposed to such methods, not only because of their loss of control and the intensification of the pace of work, but also because of the inevitable loss of quality which they have always regarded as integral to their skill. The desired rate of output, or standard 100 performance, which is to be 'naturally achieved', is encouraged by a bonus payment. Not one that necessarily rewards increased output, but one which penalises lower output by a drop in wages. Although it need not be the case, the introduction of a standard performance can mean a reduction in wages as the system is widely abused. A woman describes what happened in her factory: 'Some of the girls were earning reasonable money before it was "engineered", now their wages are out by about £10 a week.'

Some clothing employers 'claw back' wage agreements by setting an impossibly high standard performance. A standard performance is based on capability tests which can be used to push and push at what can be naturally achieved. A supervisor, Mavis Hall, explains how they are done:

You see you get a works study – I suppose you know about that – capability tests and that, but when work study has a capability they do it on say 20 or 40 garments at a time, and they set an amount that they can do in that time. Well that's alright you might get a good high performance out of that person, but you have to do that 8 hours a day, 5 days a week, keeping that pace up. It's impossible, nobody can be expected to work at that rate.

A standard performance is not being based on what can be achieved over a working week, or a working day, but over little more than an hour. The result of this abuse of capability tests, as Mavis Hall points out, is the most appalling conditions of work:

I think it's getting worse, it's getting harder and harder each year and I'm glad I'm not on the machines because I don't think I could cope with what they've got to do. You'll get one girl and she's sewing labels on pockets all day, that's all she does all day. The numbers they have to do now are outrageous I think. Now before, that girl had about 240 labels per hour to sew on, now she has 390. They've fixed certain attachments to the machine and they say it's quicker, so they put the numbers up. Now I know I'm going to flog those girls to death to get that number out.

Women: the Backbone of the Industry

This intensification of work is not by any means confined to back street sweatshops, rather it is the 'normal' practice of 'modern' factories. The industry exerts this kind of pressure on women because, despite some technological change, it remains locked in its characteristically labour-intensive production methods. Clothing remains dependent on some female skills whereas men's jobs have been deskilled and transformed by the introduction of machinery (See Coyle, 1982, for a fuller discussion of this). Women's labour is needed both because of the nature of the industry's products, which is constantly changing, and the nature of the labour process, which is still difficult to mechanise or automate. At the same time, because the industry has been so successful in cheapening women's labour, there is little incentive to invest in machinery to do the work now undertaken by women. This maintains clothing as a low capital industry; labour intensive, with a low rate of productivity. The ongoing dependence on women's labour as cheap labour exacerbates all the problems of low productivity, yet it seems a vice which the industry cannot escape from: '[Clothing] is caught in a vicious circle of low added value, relatively low wages, labour shortages and inability to increase output, which at one and the same time makes it difficult to take the necessary steps to raise productivity and yet which it can only break out of by a major and sudden step up in productivity' (Clothing, National Economic Development Office (NEDO), 1974, reported in *Garment Worker*, April 1975, p. 2). In this industry the economics of large-scale production and high capital investment in machinery, have not necessarily made sense. Seasonal fashion changes mean that long production runs are difficult to achieve and often undesirable. Clothing has to operate mainly on the basis of short production runs, very little stockpiling, and needs to be very responsive to market changes. Production therefore has to be very flexible and this has been achieved through the flexibility of labour. Investment in machinery can have enormous pay-offs in terms of increased productivity: in menswear, which has been less susceptible to fashion change, there has been considerable investment. But it is not relevant for the whole of the industry, nor for the whole of the production process. The intricate capabilities and flexibility of human labour cannot easily be replaced by machines and it is women's *skills* on which the industry still depends. Women provide an irresistible combination of flexibility and skill and cheapness, whilst machinery is expensive and inflexible. For the time being at least, many operations undertaken by women have retained an irreducible element of skill:

As early as 1976, Singer introduced an industrial sewing machine, the Centurion, with a memory capable of storing and repeating more than a hundred different sewing tasks at the touch of an illuminated control panel. This machine can 'learn' a sewing task from a skilled operator going once through the process which would normally have to be repeated for each article produced. If widely adopted, such a machine would appear to have major implications both for employment levels and for the skills required of clothing workers. However, no evidence has so far emerged that it is being adopted and sources in the industry are sceptical about the likelihood of its replacing traditional methods in the near future, giving both technical and economic reasons for their views. It is argued that a reduction in machining time is relatively unimportant compared with the time spent in handling fabric and positioning it ready to be

11

machined, something for which no technical substitute for human skills has yet been discovered; that the machine would not be able to 'ease' together two edges of fabric of slightly different lengths, as a skilled human operator can (however accurate the electronic cutting, fabric will continue to shrink and expand variably as the result of changes in temperature and humidity); and that many of the small firms which make up a large proportion of the industry . . . are unlikely to be in a position to invest in new technology. (Ursula Huws, 1980, p. 58.)

As early as 1946, a Board of Trade investigation into the clothing industry detailed the relative backwardness of the industry rooted in its low-capital technical base and labour-intensive production process. Throughout the 1950s and 1960s, successive governments allocated grants to the industry and in 1975, on the recommendations of the Economic Development Council for Clothing, large capital grants were made available for equipping and training. The take up of such incentives has been uneven and has not shifted the labour-intensive basis of the industry. Relocation grants, on the other hand, have been taken up with some enthusiasm. They have provided the possibility for the industry to move to new pastures. Away from traditional clothing areas, where labour was becoming well organised and resistant to deskilling; to coal-mining areas, such as South Wales and Yorkshire, where there were no alternative employment opportunities for women, and where miners' wives provided a ready supply of unskilled 'green' labour (Community Development Project/CDP, 1977, p. 74).

In 1976, capital expenditure per employee was still lower than for any other manufacturing industry: £2,928 per head, compared with £6,089 per head for all manufacturing industry (Business Statistics Office, 1976). Productivity has increased at a rate faster than any other manufacturing industry, but output per employee is still only half of that for all manufacturing industry. The rate of improvement really indicates the room for improvement, and the industry still places an emphasis on the intensification of work, rather than technical investment, as the way of increasing productivity.

12

The Symptoms of Decline

Imports

No matter how work study is used to intensify the labour process and to increase productivity, the clothing industry in the UK has not been able to produce garments anywhere near as cheaply as its rival foreign counterparts. Since the war, clothing has become a major industry for many developing countries and they have a major advantage of significantly lower labour costs. They operate mostly under conditions of non-unionisation and are able to exert a degree of control over production that is not achievable in the UK (Elson and Pearson, 1981). It means that producers in Hong Kong and Taiwan, for example, can price their finished garments at a cost that would only buy the cloth in Britain (*Garment Worker*, June 1975). Import penetration deepened especially throughout the 1970s, to the extent that some retail markets appear permanently lost to foreign producers. Now, for example, three-quarters of all shirts sold in Britain are imported. There is a persistent call for import controls from within the industry as a way of saving the British clothing trade, but import controls do in fact already operate. The first set of curbs on imports from the Third World and South East Asia were established in 1961 which limited the quantity of imported cotton goods. In 1973 these restrictions were extended in the Multi-Fibre Arrangement (MFA) to include man-made fibres, both textiles and garments. The original intention of such controls was to give the industry a period of respite from competition in which it could become more efficient and competitive. It was intended very much to be a temporary measure but in fact was renewed in 1977 and most recently in 1981, and now import restrictions have been in operation for 20 years. Without such controls there would have been even greater job loss, but they are not effective in any sense. They serve only to maintain an ailing industry rather than facilitate its modernisation. Nor have they succeeded in really restricting imports. Many foreign producers have been able to manipulate their export quotas, or to find their way around them with false labelling and false certificates of origin. In the end, however, it must be recognised that import controls are not the answer to the clothing industry's problems, nor are the short-comings of import controls the cause of the industry's demise. Some rival producers are not from the low wage economies of the Third World but from West Germany and Scandinavia, which are more technically advanced and more efficient. In fact the UK industry has the lowest labour costs in the EEC. As more and more competitors join the EEC, such as Sweden and Turkey, import controls will become an increasingly inappropriate strategy.

Homework and Sweatshops

In recession homework is flourishing. The clothing industry has always drawn upon the labour of homeworkers. The low technical composition of the labour process means that the production process is so flexible, it is *mobile*. Homework can cheapen the costs of labour because it places the labour force outside of the protection of factory legislation or union organisation. There was a discernible movement away from homeworkers in the 1930s both because factory production became more efficient and because it is difficult to control the quality of work that is contracted out. The practice has never disappeared however, rather it has co-existed with factory production. In the 1980s, homeworkers are once more a flourishing form of production. The real extent of homeworking is impossible to measure. Its almost invisibility is part of its attraction. Women working at home are cheap, flexible and technically self-employed. They have no employment or wage protection. It is without doubt a most exploitative form of labour, drawing upon women who for one reason or another are unable to get employment (Cragg and Dawson, 1981; Hope *et al.*, 1976). The London fashion trade has always made use of outwork and homework, but it was recently estimated that half of that trade is now produced by women working at home (Campbell, 1979).

Like homeworking, 'sweatshops' are also proliferating in recession. They are no new phenomenon to the industry which has always supported this sort of underbelly. They appear to do well in difficult economic times. They can be set up on little capital and

14

provide the market for cheap clothing. Since the early 1970s, many such factories are Asian owned and employ almost entirely Asian women. This expansion has arisen through the influx of Asian immigrants to Britain who have skills in garment manufacture and few alternative opportunities. Racial discrimination has forced both employer and employee into a particularly self-contained system of production. Their existence is very precarious. Bankruptcy and closure are frequent, but as one factory closes down, another replaces it. Asian producers draw upon an especially vulnerable labour force – Asian women. As immigrant women they will find it extremely difficult to get any other sort of work, and they often enter such jobs with little or no previous work experience and little knowledge of employment rights. Often female labour is recruited through personal, family and community networks and, because of that, a degree of control over the labour force can be achieved which goes far beyond the usual wage bargain. Women are bound to their employers in a personalised way and are often steeped in obligation to them. Asian employers are often unwilling to employ white women because they can only be controlled by the wage rather than this personal obligation (Hoel, 1982).

The problems facing union organisation for such women are enormous. A producer's very existence is often premised on the fact that the workforce is paid as little as half the going rate. Moreover such producers are totally responsive to the market and need to shorten or lengthen the working day as needs be, and are able to do without earnings' protection or overtime payment (ibid.). Despite the difficulties they face, Asian women have not been totally passive victims of such exploitation and indeed have displayed great strength and commitment in their struggles, including fighting for trade union recognition both in clothing and other industries. The needs of such women place extra demands on local trade union officials who cannot, or perhaps do not want to, cope with them. It is perceived as a major problem by the Garment Workers' Union but to begin to deal with the problem they will have to go far beyond their usual activities. For at the moment they appear to be somewhat out of their depth.

Strategies for Survival

The clothing industry still has a seemingly irreducible dependence on women's skills. The micro-electronic technology now available to the industry has finally killed any remaining elements of men's cutting skills and could provide an advantage for some firms over competitors. Where computerised cutting is in operation, its effects are staggering. Hepworths, who are pioneering suit cutting with computerised cutting control, have invested two million pounds in such equipment and reckon they have improved productivity on their made-to-measure suits by 250 percent (Trade Union Community Resource and Information Centre/TUCRIC, 1980). Not only has this new technology affected the final obsolescence of men's craft skills, but it has become women's work. Hepworths' equipment serves all their retail outlets and is operated by a team of six women working on two shifts. Cutting is now an operation that is essentially controlled by computer, it requires a short training and is designated a semi-skilled operation. However, such technology is very expensive, entailing massive capital outlay which is beyond the resources of the smaller and 'typical' clothing firm.[4] Only the very largest of companies with secure retail outlets are undertaking this kind of investment. Moreover, new cutting equipment does not significantly diminish the labour-intensive nature of the industry because men as cutters represent a relatively small proportion of the labour force (12 percent).

Some firms have combined technical changes with new marketing strategies. One such strategy has been to move upmarket – not to attempt to compete in terms of price of garment, but to produce high quality garments under exclusive labels. Both Austin Reed and Hepworths are producing and selling expensive clothes for the expensive man, but even here foreign producers have moved into the market. Mujani designer jeans, promoted by Blondie, are made in Hong Kong, as is menswear, produced under franchise for the ultimate name in *haute couture*, Yves St. Laurent.

Retail markets are crucial in the life of the clothing industry and if the British industry has any future the links between retailer and manufacturer must consolidate further. Marks & Spencer has been a very significant agent in the clothing industry and they have shown how this relationship could develop. Without them the industry would have been even further in decline. Marks & Spencer's policy of buying British has arisen out of commercial necessity rather than any soft sentiment (Hird *et al.*, 1980). It has found a very successful retail market by selling guaranteed quality at reasonable prices. It can only maintain that quality by having very close links with its producers and exercising very tight controls over their production methods. For Marks & Spencer to be able to exercise that kind of control, producers have to be, on the whole, near to home. In this alliance between manufacturer and retailer, clothing manufacturers benefit enormously from Marks & Spencer's forward planning in production and retail, and get the nearest they can to a stable run. However, companies such as Marks & Spencer are first and foremost pursuing their own interests and profits and can be equally responsible for the 'sudden death' of a firm if they decide to terminate their contract (Campbell, 1979).

Over the last five years there has been a noticeable trend for firms to amalgamate. Such economic concentration of the industry could provide the capital resources necessary for future development. But recession does not provide the ideal circumstance for restructuring and the same economic conditions which have forced many companies to combine and seek shelter in each other's arms, also open the way to increased import penetration and the proliferation of sweatshops, outwork and homework.

Rather than leading the way forward to a revitalised industry, some of the biggest clothing manufacturers have now opted to reduce or close down altogether their manufacturing commitments and to concentrate instead on retail. Burton, for example, reduced their manufacturing operations from ten to three factories, but retained their biggest asset, their high street shops. They run 300 Burton shops, 20 Jackson the Tailor, 80 Evans, 2 Peter Robinson, 50 Top Man and 70 Top Shops; and in 1979 they acquired Dorothy Perkins. In 1980 their trade levels were up 20 percent and their profits trebled. In that same year, those retail outlets carried only 50 percent of the output from their own factories and the rest was purchased on foreign markets. Hepworths have similarly made many closures in their manufacturing operations but have expanded in the high street with 300 retail outlets and record profits for 1979, 26 percent up on the previous year (TUCRIC, 1980). What has occurred is a structural shift from clothing manufacture to clothing retail. The largest firms are not disappearing, they are simply moving their interests but contributing to the growth in the sale of imported clothing. In a similar vein, some of the larger manufacturers have closed down factories and sub-contracted work out (Haringey and Lewisham Women's Employment Project, 1981), turning a blind eye to how garments are produced (Campbell, 1979). Now the most respected of chain stores and clothes shops sell clothing made by women working at home.

The official preoccupation of the industry over the last three decades has been with 'modernisation' and 'development', recognising its own relative backwardness and the underlying problem of low productivity. The Economic Development Council for the clothing industry has long sought not only technical development but decent pay and conditions. Low pay causes high labour turnover costing the industry over £15 million a year (Clothing Economic Development Council, 1967). Yet in practice the industry cannot make the transition of providing decent pay and conditions for women. The introduction of high technology has been combined with and maintained all the intensive, exploitative conditions of work, associated with the industry. But there is no reason why it should be otherwise, clothing exploits existing inequalities and has incorporated the subordination of women into its own economic existence.

Clothing cannot be taken to be typical of women's work, although it is probably the trade most associated with women. Rather, the conditions for women in clothing present an enlarged version of all the problems women face in employment: low pay and a non-recognition of women's skills. Because of clothing's specific need to cheapen labour, it still forces forms of exploitation not dissimilar to nineteenth-century forms of production and 'sweating'. In recession the rate of job loss amongst women in the industry has increased. This is partly due to increases in labour productivity, but mostly because clothing manufacturers have drastically scaled down their operations, or gone out of business altogether. Where jobs exist the conditions of employment have significantly deteriorated, but so have women's employment opportunities. Those women who remain in the industry are there because they have nowhere else to go.

2
Redundancy

This book is about the impact of redundancy and unemployment on the lives of a number of female clothing workers who lost their jobs when the factories in which they were employed closed down. This chapter is an account of the background to those closures and the predominantly female workforce's response to it. It outlines how one company resorted to 'surgery' – a euphemistic metaphor for a drastic restructuring programme and job loss – as a strategy for survival in recession. It also indicates how the response of women to redundancy has to be understood in terms of a *mesh* of social relations, production, the family and gender, and not in terms of some simple notion of femininity or of women's domestic role.

A Strategy for Recession

The Harrogate and Castleford factories were two factories which closed in December 1980, shedding their entire production workforce, belonged to the clothing manufacturing firm of Roger Firth. Best known perhaps for its regulation school raincoats, its factories have always produced a range of menswear both under its own labels and under contract for the big chain stores. The firm was established in the early 1950s and expanded to five factories, despite the unstable conditions of the industry, by producing and finding a market for fairly standardised men's garments: the classic men's overcoats, raincoats, jackets and trousers which, despite the whims of fashions, maintained an element of certainty. Nothing, however, stays the same forever and by the early 1970s fashion began to creep into even the mainstream of men's clothing.

Many British males abandoned their overcoats and suits and instead began to clothe themselves in sports coats, anoraks, bomber jackets and jeans. Roger Firth found themselves in a situation of increased competition, falling sales and no capital resources to be able to respond to change. Their crisis was resolved in 1974 by merging with Carrington Viyella, the textile conglomerate, who offered capital and breathing space to rethink their product range and to rationalise production with some investment in new equipment. They moved cautiously into a more fashionable, casual range of men's jackets and trousers and here they found some success, even though short-time working remained an occasional necessity.

The merger with Carrington Viyella, however, had other implications. Having pursued policies of expansion, diversification and takeover in the 1970s, Carrington Viyella ended up as an organisation consisting of a wide range of not only diverse but often overlapping and competing divisions. Some of Roger Firth's traditional market rivals, for example, had also become part of the Carrington Viyella empire. By 1980, this empire was in great difficulties and embarked upon a programme of reorganisation, rationalisation and restructuring, and because of the overlapping divisions which had been created, it meant a transformation of the entire structure of the organisation: manufacturing, marketing, retail distribution and administration. Operating under heavy losses and huge borrowing commitments, the company decided to take 'firm action'. Following a plan drawn up by an American Business Consultancy, it sought a strategy for survival. Inevitably this meant contracting fast, and the last quarter of 1980 and all of 1981 saw an extraordinary programme of closures and redundancy:

Carrington Viyella, best known for its up-market menswear and household linens, yesterday announced a huge net loss of £31.6 million for 1980. Squeezed between a flood of cheap imports and reduced home demand, Carrington Viyella has made savage cuts in an effort to survive. Nearly half of its 113 operating sites in Britain have been closed or shrunk and over a quarter of its workforce – 6,400 employees – have been sacked.

A further 1,000 jobs will go before the group completes its closure plans. . . . Carrington Viyella's £31.6 million deficit is unlikely to be repeated since most of it came in closure costs of £21.5 million. (*Guardian*, 26 February 1981.)

The Harrogate and Castleford closures and the hundreds of jobs lost there were only a fraction of the thousands of jobs lost during this period of restructuring.

One year on, Carrington Viyella's programme of radical 'surgery' offered the group the promise of a future.

Optimism over the prospects for the Carrington Viyella textiles group as a result of the drastic reorganisation and rationalisation programme undertaken in the past two years was expressed by the chairman, Bill Fieldhouse, at the annual meeting yesterday. Mr Fieldhouse said that Carrington Viyella would benefit in 1982 from the actions taken in 1981. . . . In the past year operations at 14 sites had been closed down and reduced in scale on another four sites. In the period 1980–81 a total of 55 sites had either been closed down or rationalised, an indication of the scale of surgery which the group, whose very survival was in question two years ago, has undergone. . . . In 1981 the demands of extricating the group from the legacy of the past had detracted from its capacity to develop new business but the board was now confident that this transformation had now been completed. (*Guardian*, 11 March 1982.)

The final decision to close the Castleford and Harrogate factories had not been made until the autumn of 1980 and during that year a range of plans and proposals were mooted, as Roger Chambers, a Roger Firth director explains:

The point was the plans changed so much anyway, they didn't have a master plan, they had many master plans, at every meeting they changed their minds. And it wasn't just the fact that they didn't know what they were doing, although there was a lot of that, it was people trying to fit themselves into the new

22

structure and if it didn't suit them personally, they would of course be against it. And some of the closures were made on such sketchy information. We had a firm of American consultants, and they came round and interviewed everybody and went to all the units, and I had to give them a run down of all the factories that I'd been connected with, and I was with them I would think about an hour, and I'm sure much of what I said was used because nobody else knew about things as intimately as I did, and I consider that this bright 25-year-old American, took away this information and it was on this kind of rather sketchy, chatty information, that factories were closed, it's really frightening. No doubt they would say that my information was just a little piece of a jigsaw. . . .

The Harrogate factory was the administrative headquarters of the Roger Firth firm, as well as the site for the manufacturing of overcoats and jackets. It had been in operation for over 25 years and the 'home' of Roger Firth. Of the five factories in the firm, it was the last to be 'engineered' and was very inefficient. Right up to the time of closure new work methods were being introduced, but the workforce there, predominantly older, skilled men and women, were resistant to those changes. There had been plans to transform Harrogate and to make it into one of two administrative centres for Carrington Viyella, to produce a small output of high quality garments and to utilise the skills of the workforce, but in the end such plans came to nothing. As Peter Chambers explained:

[At one point] Carrington Viyella had decided to have two administrative headquarters . . . one in Manchester and one in Yorkshire, and Harrogate seemed to be the right place to have the Yorkshire one because it was already set up. Carrington Viyella had decided to structure the marketing in two ways. First of all they were going to have a Marks & Spencer operation and then an own-brand operation which would be quite distinct – 'own brand' meaning our own sales force going out to sell to individual shops our own brand. So different personnel would run these two headquarters and it seemed logical that they should be separate. And then unfortunately for the plans the managing director of Roger Firth, who was the king pin in all of this, decided that he couldn't go along with being the 'own brand' managing director because he didn't think the structure would work, so he tendered his resignation, and then the plans changed and then they moved the whole plant to Manchester, to two different places in Manchester.

The decision to close the Harrogate factory and offices was finally arrived at through a range of different criteria. It was not operating efficiently and the site which they owned, unlike others which were rented, would have some market value. It was off the main trunk road network. Additionally, the management team at Harrogate were long used to being 'the bosses' and were not easily drawn into the new structure of Carrington Viyella. No matter what their new titles were within the Carrington Viyella group they would cease to be in charge of their own firm and their non-co-operation contributed to the failure to devise any alternative and workable proposals for Harrogate's future.

The criteria for closing the Castleford factory had been quite different from those applying to Harrogate. Within the group of factories, the Castleford factory was regarded as a model of efficiency and the young manager there, the blue-eyed boy of the firm. It was a 'lovely little factory', small and efficient, producing about 3,000 trousers a week. It had been in operation for about ten years. Its labour force was much younger than Harrogate, all women and less skilled. Castleford was closed in order to expand and concentrate the production of trousers in one place. Production was transferred from Castleford to a factory at Tadcaster, a new site owned by Carrington Viyella with the physical space to make long-term expansion possible: 'I'll tell you the official line, it was that Castleford was a small factory producing 3,000 pairs of trousers a week; not a million miles away at Tadcaster, there is another factory which potentially could produce 11 or 12,000 pairs of trousers, but is currently producing 5,000, so its seems logical if you want to maximise the potential of one of the factories, it's got to be Tadcaster' (Peter Chambers).

But Ian Grant, the former manager of Castleford, considered capacity was only one aspect of the decision-making process:

When it came to making trousers it boiled down to a choice between Tadcaster and Castleford. . . . Now, on almost every count, Castleford scored over Tadcaster. It was more efficient, however you measure efficiency. Whether it was on the numbers of garments produced, the number of people who produced them, the quality of work, work in progress. . . . But at that time Carrington Viyella were desperately trying to get into the Marks & Spencer market in trousers. We do a lot with M & S, but nothing in trousers. We had made them at Castleford for M & S, but M & S didn't like the Castleford factory because it was small and a bit grubby and the ladies toilets weren't really up to M & S standards, the canteen wasn't very clean and they didn't like the cook . . . that sort of thing. Castleford just wasn't an M & S type of factory, but this (Tadcaster) is. The toilets are reasonable. . . . It's a nice little town to come and visit and Castleford isn't. Also at that time capacity came into it. This is quite a big factory with a theoretical output of 12 to 15,000 trousers per week, depending on the type of garment. Castleford's capacity was maybe 5,000, so you're talking about at least three times as much. Being optimistic they plumped for Tadcaster.

The Climate of Redundancy

After the 1980 summer break, the Harrogate factory went on to short-time working as unsold garments piled up in the stockroom, but neither this nor the proliferation of rumours of closure, nor the knowledge of widespread closures elsewhere, prepared the way for the event. Management had 'engineered' (reorganised) the factory and although it was on an impossibly low budget, this put off fears and suspicions: 'We just started to reorganise the Harrogate factory, and people were saying, as they always do, when we were doing it, that they wouldn't be spending money on reorganising if they were going to close the place. And I knew differently, but I had to go along with it and do my best to carry out with enthusiasm the task which I had been set' (work study director).

The first move towards redundancy – although few, including the union appeared to read it as such – occurred one month before the closures were announced. The management of Roger Firth called in the area representative of the National Union of Tailors and Garment Workers and announced that they were no longer going to be bound by the wage agreement that they had settled at Harrogate with the introduction of new work methods. This agreement had been very important because it guaranteed that new work methods would not be a device for reducing wages. It guaranteed machinists the maintenance of their previous earnings levels. Production at Harrogate had long been based on a form of piece-work, whereby fast operators could make up good wages. But Proficiency Payment Schemes introduced with work study can be an abuse of work study and a form of reducing wages, where payment does not increase proportionately to productivity, and actually decreases in relation to productivity so that once a fast operator reaches the maximum efficiency of the standard 100 performance, after that she earns proportionately less (see Alexander, 1980). Roger Firth had continued to pay a guarantee of previous earnings – as a way of trying to make the new methods of work they were introducing more acceptable to the workforce. The fact that the guarantee existed at all says quite a lot about Roger Firth's style of management. They regarded it as an acceptable cost for increased productivity. The work study director could be quite ruthless in his application of 'scientific' technique but he did not consider wage cutting part of that:

> Just before the news broke, and I'm talking of within a month of the news breaking, we got the union representative in and we withdrew this agreement. . . . The high earners are people with more than 100 performance. We know that an operator who used to be a big earner, will not be a 100 performer she'll be 110 or 115 performer and so they got an increase by those 15 points. . . . The idea was to save money per unit, not that wage costs should be lower . . . by doing more for the same wage bill or a

slightly higher wage bill. Which I think is acceptable, in my terms it's acceptable, I can go along with that, but I can't go along with the fact that the wage bill is going to be cut. . . . I disassociated myself from this in front of the union, I said I wanted no part of this and that I would do as I was told, but somebody else would have to tell the operators because I wasn't going to do something I disagreed with. So this we did, we got all the operators into the canteen and the production director (usually I would do this kind of thing) he had to do it.

This ending of the guaranteed earnings agreement affected the *women* and one by one they were called into the personnel office, where they were asked to sign a new agreement. The union did not oppose it, nor did they offer the women any advice or support over what they should do. A supervisor explained: 'They went on to a different piece-work scheme, the time and motion thing was different and you hadn't any choice, the unions said we had to go on it. The idea was to do more work for less money, which of course didn't go down well. . . .' Only one woman refused to sign it and she was, in fact, one of the two shop stewards at Harrogate. Whilst she fully appreciated its implications, she perceived herself in an individual struggle with management over it, and was prepared to leave rather than sign a new agreement. She never perceived it as an issue for collective or union action:

Yes, we had to work a lot harder – I mean you worked hard normally but you had to work even harder. They gave you so long to build up your speed, then they would take you in the office and say you had to sign like a new contract. . . . They had me in the office twice and tried to get me to sign a new contract, but I refused and I was prepared to leave rather than sign. . . . A lot of them signed it and it was a shame really. They lost out on their redundancy and that.

This new agreement had been accepted by the area union representative, so for this woman, or indeed any of the other women, to take it up as anything other than an individual issue would have meant taking on the union as well as management. The significance of this withdrawal of the wage agreement, which guaranteed previous earning levels, meant that the subsequent redundancy payments could be calculated on the basis of the *reduced* weekly earnings of the operators.

Breaking the News

The redundancies were officially announced on 2 December 1980 and by 19 December, both the Castleford and Harrogate factories had ceased operations. The union area representative was informed of the closures over dinner just days before the official notification. There was no question of consultation or negotiation. Management regarded the union as weak:

> There was nothing much the trade union could do. The redundancy terms were better than minimum. Instead of the normal week per year it was a week and a half. They got pay in lieu of notice even though there was some notice. So the redundancy terms were, if not generous, a bit better than minimum. I think the union in this industry is a bit shell-shocked anyway. It's just something that they accept. It's just something that happens every day.

The local trade union official shared that view, and the most that could be hoped for was a reasonable redundancy package: 'We got a good deal. We've got no muscle, but you see, we're nearly all women.'

Employees at Harrogate received ten weeks' payment in lieu of notice and were paid up until 2 March 1981, whilst employees at Castleford received four weeks' payment in lieu of notice and were paid up until 2 January 1981. Most, but not all, were entitled to redundancy pay and holiday pay. The manufacture of coats and jackets was transferred from Harrogate to Roger Firth, Northern Ireland, and the trousers from Castleford to Carrington Viyella's factory at Tadcaster. Management were relocated to other factories within the company, but often under conditions of demotion and with no more advance warning than production workers. Some of the more senior management resigned from the company.

The official notification ended an extremely unsettling and demoralising year for the Harrogate workforce. They had seen the introduction of new work methods, time and motion study, a new wage agreement, short-time working and finally closure:

I think what spoiled Roger Firth in my opinion, in the first place, was the time and motion men, they killed it. Everybody was happy until then, everybody was earning a decent wage and they were putting more heart into it. Then they got these time and motion men and they were at the young ones to do more. Of course they could do more but it wasn't half done, and the young didn't know whether they were coming or going. They couldn't reckon up, they couldn't figure out the points in numbers. Some left and got other jobs. Half of those young ones were real good little workers. They'd have been good tailoresses. Well I think that started the trouble.

Well after we came back off our holiday, we had two weeks off for summer holiday, and they said when we come back that we had another week. I remember the week's holiday and the government had to pay us that week, and then after we came back off our holidays we started doing short time, like three days a week, and it went on like that until we got nearly to the end of November. We were slacking really out and it went down to one day a week. We were making jackets but we weren't selling them. Then about three weeks before Christmas we got told we were going to be made redundant and we were all called to the cutting room and told there. It was really awful. I came home and told me mum and she couldn't believe it. She said, 'Well why does it have to be our factory?'

We didn't know anything exactly, for a year there was talk, same as everywhere else. Work was slacking off, then they started taking people on but we could see that there was no work for these people they were taking on. Nobody said anything officially and if any of us asked – 'Oh! A load of rubbish' – you know, to put us off. It went on for a whole year, people were getting fed up and you could see the girls weren't doing their work properly. Their attitude was 'why bother they're only in the store room'. They could see the store room filling up with coats, not being sold. Well it was getting pretty evident when they started on the three-day week. . . . Some of the girls got so that they didn't want to come in – if there was a bit of work and it was their two days off, they'd say: 'Oh! Do you really want me to come in?'. They'd say, 'Oh! It's not fair, I was in last week. Why can't so and so come in?'

Castleford had not had the same kind of forewarnings: 'Castleford had always been extolled by everybody as being a lovely little factory, very efficient and very good quality, and nobody could believe that they could be so stupid as to close that, but they did. So I think that they were stunned when the news came out' (Peter Chambers). But clothing workers are used to working intensively, at high speed, and under pressure. So that for them, the first sign of trouble is inevitably a 'slacking off' of that pressure, and that did not happen: 'The work stopped all of a sudden and things don't stop like that, it runs down. We only found out afterwards that work was being detoured to this other factory.' They had their suspicions but in the end redundancy is always a shock:

When they started to empty the warehouse you know there's something fishy going on. And we couldn't find out anything, nothing at all, though I think we worked ourselves out of a job, I think our output was too much. I kept saying to the manager 'we're working ourselves out of a job here' because I know for a fact that at one time we had rows and rows of trousers waiting for coats. So I got an inkling then. . . . Yes I think we were all amazed because the output was so good and we kept getting praise from head office. I think we were all amazed when it came.

You never think that you'll be made redundant. You think it'll pick up.

A Postscript

It is with irony and some bitterness that former employees of Roger Firth have been able to chart the outcome of Carrington Viyella's decisions. The factory at Tadcaster which had taken on Castleford's work was beset with problems. To quote one ex-manager:

Tadcaster's doing just trousers. But whereas the potential is 11,000 or 12,000, they're actually doing 5,000, so that place is a 'white elephant'. They've currently got about five production engineers trying to reorganise it and some of them I know personally and they're good guys, but at the same time as trying to reorganise it, they're having to make all kinds of funny styles, and each time they have the stall set out there's a new style comes in, so there's been no value engineering, which is the rationalisation of styles so that small variations can be accommodated into a kind of uniform product. That hasn't been done, nor is it intended to be done, so it's going to be very, very difficult to get that place efficient.

The former factory manager of Castleford, who was transferred to Tadcaster, has been experiencing the problems at first hand and explained why expansion had been anticipated:

Well they'd just closed Reliant slacks, and they did about 3,000 a week, and they'd closed Castleford doing 3,000, so there's 6,000. At that time this place was doing about 5,000 a week. So they thought that they could pack it all into one. In fact practically all of Reliant's trade went. Actually most of the work that we do here now is what we did at Castleford. It's the Tadcaster work that we've lost. Tadcaster was quite well in, and did a lot of work for C & A and Burtons, but there's hardly any work for C & A now and none for Burtons. We didn't get the

31

M & S contract. Most of the work we do here is Roger Firth's work. It's galling really.

The market for men's trousers has, in fact, contracted further and existing markets have been lost.

The greatest irony of all, perhaps, was that Tadcaster had a problem of labour shortage and one which had never been anticipated. Although clothing has always been beset by the problems of labour shortage and high labour turnover, in recent years employers have enjoyed an unusually stable labour supply because of a contracting job market. 'Traditionally that's been the thing that as soon as there's been a crunch – they don't like the rates, or they fall out with the supervisor – off they go, but in the last couple of years, the labour turnover in all our factories has really fallen' (Peter Chambers). Carrington Viyella at Tadcaster had always managed to recruit locally, about 30 female production workers but, after having rebuilt and expanded the factory, they were forced to draw labour from a much wider area.

> Labour is a hell of a problem here. I can't think why they built a factory here in the first place. It's a nice town but the labour just isn't here and there's no tradition of it either. . . . Most of the people who work here, we have to bus in from Leeds, York, Garforth, and even Castleford. Going back 12 months, we used to provide free transport and that was costing us about £30,000 a year and we couldn't keep it up. So we have to charge the girls, and they pay for it themselves. It's still subsidised to some extent, but not a lot. (Ian Grant.)

So desperate did labour shortage become that early in 1981, Carrington Viyella ended up re-employing some of the women they had laid off just a few months previously. Ian Grant approached some of his former 'girls' and asked them to try working in Tadcaster. Quite a few did, although as one woman illustrates, it was more out of loyalty for their former boss, than anything else: 'He kept ringing me and ringing me, asking me to go to Tadcaster. He kept on and on and I think I did it more out of loyalty to him, he'd always been very good to me. It's four pounds something a week on the bus, and it's a lot longer day than before, a lot longer.' After six months, most had left again. The travelling, especially in winter, became a strain, the conditions of work became harder and harder, and those that remained were there because they had little choice: 'To be truthful I don't think I shall stay there much longer either, I'm very discontented. All the girls are fed up, but they're in a funny position. They can't put in their notices because they can't get jobs, but I know they would if they could.' Moreover the threat of closure remained, as a manager at Tadcaster reveals: 'The sales aren't there to support what we're producing and I anticipate that we'll be on short time, or there'll be redundancies here. We could even close down. Of course, Carrington Viyella would like to get out of manufacturing altogether . . . that's the way things are going.' In July 1982, the Tadcaster factory did indeed close down. The Harrogate factory site remains empty and unsold.

Women and Redundancy

There is a thesis that women are more passive than men in redundancy, and therefore more vulnerable to it (see Wood, 1981). That women have a less committed relation to work and are ambivalent about job loss because their lives straddle work and family, and implicitly are more rooted in the latter. This idea informs the few accounts there are of job loss amongst women: 'After all, they were always highly ambivalent about their right to work – the young wanting to escape, the older ones riddled with contradictions and guilt. . . . Half in the home, half in the factory, most women only needed a small shove to regard themselves as full-time housewives' (Pollert, 1982, p. 228). There can be little doubt that employers do select women to go first in redundancy, but whether they do so in the knowledge of feminine passivity and ambivalence or because women are invariably less protected in their jobs than men, and thereby are easier and cheaper to dispose of (see Chapter 6) is a moot point. Undoubtedly most women

33

who have lost their jobs have done so without *visible* protest, but there have been women who have refused to go, and then found themselves in a situation where they are fighting their employers, their union and the men they work alongside (Vaughan, 1981). The fact that this happens at all suggests that any simple explanation of women's 'acceptance' of redundancy, rooted in femininity or their domestic role will not do, and women's responses to redundancy have to be understood in the total context of work, family *and men*; men as managers, trade unionists, shop floor workers and husbands.

The redundancies at Roger Firth occurred through the total closure of two factories, and the dismissal of almost all the workforce, men and women. There was never any question of women going first, in preference to men. In this instance, men and women were finally treated equally in their redundancy, with the same redundancy terms and entitlement. Indeed, on the face of it, the Redundancy Payments Scheme appears to discriminate against men. Redundancy pay is calculated on the basis of weekly wage, age and duration of employment, with a maximum ceiling set at retirement age; 65 years for men and 60 years for women. In theory, therefore, women can reach the maximum entitlement five years sooner than men. In practice, however, none of the women at Roger Firth came off better than the men, because the other criterion of wage and duration of employment negates any advantage achieved through an earlier retirement age. Women earn less than men and tend to have more interrupted and therefore shorter employment records. Very few women reach their ceiling of entitlement under the Redundancy Payments Scheme, let alone reach it five years before men. At Roger Firth, the women were cheaper to employ and cheaper to get rid of.

Both men and women at Roger Firth accepted their redundancy, in the sense that they did not consider that there was anything else they could do. Militancy and organised resistance to redundancy are exceptions rather than the rule, although some of the most hard fought and successful struggles against redundancy have, in fact, been women's. It is possible to see, however, how the circumstances and conditions of work for women at the Harrogate and Castleford factories affected the possible avenues of response open to them. The forms of trade union organisation and managerial control at work and a general lack of support from their husbands at home, would have made it very difficult for these women to rise up in arms.

Union Organisation

The National Union of Tailors and Garment Workers (NUTGW) organises the clothing industry and had total unionisation of production workers in the Castleford and Harrogate factories. Nationally, the NUTGW has the highest proportion of female membership of any union (90 percent) yet, not untypically, it is dominated by men at every level. Redundancy and closure is the most difficult situation for any union to tackle and in this case notification came late and with no question of the redundancies negotiable.

The women at both Castleford and Harrogate were very critical of their union. They shared the men's view that the NUTGW lacked 'muscle', but also that it failed to operate under the most rudimentary principles of democratic practice and communication:

> Well the union did nothing, to be truthful, it was the poorest union I've come across in any shop. When they went to meetings, they'd come back and wouldn't tell you anything. It's like a secret squad. That's why all the silly talk went round, whereas if the union had told you how it was going, there wouldn't have been silly talk, nobody knew what to believe.

> They don't work for the people on the shop floor, they work for the bosses. Going by our representative here, I once had a do with him at our factory to be truthful. He came in about a dispute, and when it came to lunch time and we wanted to know what was going on, he sat on the staff table with the manager. So I went over to him and said, 'Mr Brown, we pay your wages and

I see no reason why I should come across to you on the staff table to discuss our business.' So he said, 'Alright Mary I'll come and sit with you.' But he shouldn't have needed that. . . . He was too much in the office before he discussed with the girls; you knew it had been sorted out before he came to us. In fact he never went out unless he'd got something in his hand, either a pair of trousers, or being measured for a suit. They never told us anything. Nothing, not even our own union woman, she was just as much in the dark as we were. I mean they should have known, they usually get together with the union and discuss where redundancies are coming don't they? So either he was very slow, or he was keeping it in the dark.

As with the earlier revision of the wages agreement, they felt that the trade union had immediately accepted the fact of redundancy and then proceeded to impart fatalism to its membership.

I don't see that they ever did anything really, they just more or less told people that they had to accept it. We didn't think that was right actually, we thought they could have fought a bit more to keep part of it, because at one time they were talking about keeping a small section of it open. . . . They didn't seem to do much, they didn't fight . . . they were telling us to accept it knowing that some of the other factories, that they were more involved with, were going to be able to be kept open if ours closed. . . .

We were very angry at first and then upset when we had time to think about it. We didn't want to be made redundant, we wanted to carry on working there. In fact there was a lot of talk that we'd put up all the redundancy money together to keep it open. . . . But the union straight away started talking about redundancy money . . . they knew it had to go and that was that.

Through the fog of rumour and non-communication, many women at the Harrogate factory certainly had strong suspicions that closure was a possibility and they made repeated enquiries to both management and union to find out what was going on. Yet at no time did the union push for information, nor take initiatives to pre-empt redundancy at a time when Carrington Viyella had not formulated their final plans for reorganisation: 'It was all in the air, but we knew. It wasn't until the last couple of weeks that we knew exactly when it would be. The union was hopeless. They didn't do a thing! We asked our union representative what was happening – "Oh! We don't know". . . .' By the time the trade union had received *formal* notification of the redundancies it was just three weeks from closure and there was, indeed, very little that could be done.

On the face of it, the women at Roger Firth combined an extraordinary mix of passivity and militancy. They would not accept poor working conditions and they sought all kinds of ways to retain control over their work:

> Well I had a row one day. You see you get used to your machine and I was moved and I wanted my own machine. I won't mention any names but this particular person said 'No'. So I just blew my top, which I didn't usually do. And I said, 'That's it, I'll give it to you verbally, that's my notice', and stormed off. Anyway I went to the ladies, had a cigarette, cooled down a bit and when I got back, funnily enough my machine was there. . . .

Nor were they dismissive of trade unions. Many women held the most fundamental views on trade unionism:

> I was a Tory, always was, I believed in free enterprise and I believed you should work for what you get, this was my idea. And then I went on a factory floor and I realised just what the workers put up with and where they would be without the unions. It was like a door opening for me. I mean I couldn't care less about the unions, I wasn't interested, they were nothing but trouble. Then I realised that without a union I was absolutely nothing. . . .

It was the trade union that let them down. Because of their relative inexperience of trade unionism, they expected the union to both represent their interests and be democratic, and had none of the men's fatalism over the 'rules' of industrial relations procedure. In fact, however, all too often the union was not democratic, did not represent their interests and did not take them seriously, even though they made up the majority of the membership. All too often their issues were not regarded as the real issues. In the face of such marginalisation, the women at Roger Firth tended to by-pass the union and fought *individual* battles. And that is the problem, women's weakness is rooted not in passivity but in lack of *organisation*.

They quite rightly reject the union when it fails to represent their interests, but fail to create alternative forms of collective organisation. The female shop steward at the Harrogate factory saw clearly the implications of the new wage contract that Roger Firth introduced and, moreover, was prepared to fight against it when the union was not. But why did she regard it as only her personal battle and why did she not make this an issue for all the female membership? Why, indeed, do women let men run their union when they have numerical strength and regard the men not only as unrepresentative of their interests but oppositional to their interests?

Paternalistic Management

If the trade union did not take its female membership seriously, management did, after a fashion. They recognised that their 'girls' were the backbone of the enterprise and that it was in their interests to treat them 'properly'. The clothing industry has a very distinctive style of management. It is controlling, paternalistic, patronising and very concessionary. Employers who are in any way dependent on female labour are forced to recognise and accommodate women's needs. It is in their interests to do so (see Freeman, 1982) and in return they get a hard-working, loyal workforce:

Because I mean it was just like family up there you know, it was a great place to work for. If you were sick, you could ring up and tell them, and they'd give you a couple of days in which to get a sick note. Or if you had any bother, you could go and see the boss and say 'can I go part-time this week and next, I've got a bit of trouble that's got to be sorted out. . . .' If the kids went down with measles say, you could ring in and tell them, and they'd say well report back as soon as you can. And in the summer time they were very good, they were smashing employers, especially for women.

They were helpful in ways that the trade union was not: 'They did a good job really. We'd go to the office if we wanted to know anything and they used to tell us more than what we'd learn from the union.'

Women at Roger Firth appreciated the ways in which management took them seriously: 'He was straight, sometimes to the point of rudeness. Now I appreciate people like that. If he thought you had a good idea to put forward, he'd listen, and if you'd work, he'd do anything for you. He was very fair. He was a damn good boss. It sounds silly this, but I think people would do anything for him. He could say, I must get this, or I must get that, and you'd go all out to help.'

The women were actually *fond* of their bosses and redundancy brought women and bosses even closer together, as they shared the experience of the closure of *their* factories.

They really got on better with the factory workers at the end than at any other time. I think it came as a bit of a shock to them as well. Mr Holt worked hard trying to keep us going. From what we can gather there were some dirty tricks played. I think when they all get into these combined firms, they just don't care about you anyway. You're better off as a private firm, as we used to be – Roger Firth. But they all started taking over and to me I think that's the beginning of the end.

The boss himself, he didn't want to close. I think he was related to the Firth family, son-in-law or something. I know he cried, sobbed his heart out.

Mr McBrian, who is a very nice person, in fact he cried, it was a very upsetting experience. . . . It didn't need to go really, it was a profit-making little place, that's what's so hard about it, on both sides, on workers' and management's.

Our boss, I was very fond of him, actually, he was a nice man.

The management had always relied upon a very personalised style of management (although very one-sided, as the women would never have dreamed of reciprocating such familiarity), and in redundancy this was heightened. To see the managing director weeping was almost as disturbing as redundancy! With the closures they were sharing an experience that was seemingly out of the control of both of them. The management at Roger Firth had also been summarily treated by Carrington Viyella, transferred and sometimes demoted, and were deeply affected by the closure of the factories with which they had long been associated. The management, who were actually the ones closing the factory down, appeared as the hapless agents and themselves the victims of Carrington Viyella. In this situation militant organisation against redundancy would have been very difficult. There appeared to be no target.

It was not quite as it appeared. Management and workforce were not in the same situation. They had been compulsorily reorganised which meant both personal and work disruption and often a loss of autonomy and status, but they had not lost their jobs. The managing director in fact resigned from Roger Firth. He had been very angry over the closures. He was angry with the dismissal of the workforce whom he knew, perhaps more intimately than most managers. But ultimately he left because he was not prepared to fit into the structure of Carrington Viyella after having been Roger Firth personified. Yet his resignation seemed to seal the bond forever. He left with them and for them.

Mr Holt, he resigned over the decision to close Castleford, because he was so disgusted.

Our Mr Holt, he was one of the bitter ones. He wouldn't stay with the group. He was the chairman, he was Roger Firth, and he wouldn't stay because of the things they asked him to do.

The problem was not that women were duped by management and their 'smooth and invisible' forms of managerial control (see Pollert, 1981, p. 157) but that management – on their terms of course – took the women more seriously, and were more helpful, than the trade union or the men on the shop floor. The men at Roger Firth had been as resigned to redundancy as the women. The general response was 'there was nothing we could do', which seems to confirm Kate Purcell's argument that it is the conditions of the industry which affect possible militancy and shop floor strength, not gender (1979, p. 131). But more often than not the men blamed their helplessness on the women. 'It's nearly all women you see' was one explanation for trade union weakness and 'the trouble is the women are just out for their holiday money' was the nugget proffered by one man who had himself been out of work for over a year and was supported by his wife in full-time employment. Women were almost driven into the arms of management by men's indifference, and sometimes hostility. It would have been very strange indeed if women had perceived their interests to lie in collective organisation, in the trade union *and* with men.

In a different context, involuntary job loss has given rise to extraordinary militant and politicised action amongst women workers. In the Lee Jeans occupation in Greenock – a *cause célèbre* of the labour movement in 1981 – women did not passively and fatalistically accept their redundancies. Rather they have fought a long, sustained and well-organised campaign to save their jobs. This action was not instigated by the trade union who gave their support only after the beginning of the occupation, but rather was directed and held together by a small group of women in a way that male-dominated trade unions have failed to do (Ryan, 1981). Additionally, the action of these women found real support in their homes and community. The high level of male unemployment in the Greenock region – twice the Scottish average – meant that three-quarters of the Lee Jeans women were the breadwinners in their families (*Guardian*, 31 March 1981). They had strong economic reasons for fighting the redundancies, but also were fighting them in a climate of some support from their men.

Whereas for the women from Harrogate and Castleford, the homefront was not encouraging:

> Well my husband – he wasn't very happy for me because he knew I liked the job and I didn't want to leave, but on the other hand I think he was glad in a way because he thought it was time I stayed at home a bit, he's always been a bit like that.

> He likes me at home because he always had to do the dinners, now everything's done for him when he comes home. He was pleased. But I miss my bit of money, my own bit . . . he lets me please myself, but he likes me at home. In fact he's started coming home for his dinner now (midday), and he never used to. He nips home for an hour.

Who would have supported them in a fight for their jobs? Therefore all they could share was shock and a sense of loss.

> Let's face it, if they hadn't have made us redundant I'd never have finished because it was a job – well to me it was no trouble and I loved it. In fact I was off sick two or three days before we actually closed down, and I went in, and all our side of the factory was empty. I sat down and cried. I remember Mr Grant coming in and saying, 'We all feel like that Mary, it's no use going on like that'. And to see me weep was amazing for them because I'm a hard person, but just the impact of seeing that empty factory and knowing that you weren't going to go there and do that job any more. I don't think people realise.

You see you hear about this crisis and all these places closing but you don't realise because you're safe in your job. But when it happens to you, you think, 'Oh God!' The actual day when I finished, that's when it hit me.

3
On the Labour Market

This chapter looks at the experiences of the labour market. It follows the Roger Firth women from redundancy into their search for jobs, the conditions of the local labour market and the jobs they subsequently found. It is important to note that although they were all clothing workers, they were by no means a homogenous group. They could be differentiated by work experience and skills, age and domestic commitments. What is most striking is that their different needs were *not* accommodated by the labour market and this is contrary to the accepted wisdom that women's paid employment is fitted around their other commitments. It is women who are flexible, not employers, and in both Harrogate and Castleford women were forced into the working patterns of employers, irrespective of their individual requirements.

The First Step

After the closure of Roger Firth almost all the women from Harrogate and Castleford were back on the labour market looking for work.[5] Redundancy did not present itself as an opportunity to 'retreat' back into the family.

Registration as unemployed is the first formal step to be made in job seeking. The numbers of registered unemployed women has in fact been rising both because women are losing their jobs more rapidly and because of an increased propensity to register. Why women should now be more inclined to register is not clear, but in part it is obvious that female registration is being pushed up by a steady increase in the number of girls leaving school without work, whilst changes in the National Insurance requirements since 1977 mean that married women are no longer able to opt out of the National Insurance Scheme. More women will now register as they are able to make a claim for benefit in their own right. Moreover, registered unemployment is an index of the demand for jobs (Institute for Employment Research, University of Warwick, 1982, p. 47), and there are contradictory effects of high unemployment levels. One may be that women are discouraged from registering, but the other may be that women feel the need more than ever to stake their claim to work in a contracting labour market. The women from Roger Firth had the opportunity to register at the time of the factory closures:

> What happened was some people from the Job Centre came into the factory on our last days and gave us a little interview and put our names down on cards so we were more or less registered straight away. They gave us a card to go down the unemployment benefit place and they gave us a date after Christmas to go and sign on. They made us redundant just before Christmas and you couldn't really look for another job over Christmas. . . .

But not everyone took up this opportunity, and married women, particularly married women over 40, did not register themselves as unemployed. Many women had used the married women's option as a way of maximising their wage packets at a time when they most needed it. They had happily foregone their rights to social security benefits for the short-term trade off of a few extra pounds a week in their pay. It was only on redundancy that they were confronted with the full implications of their choice:

> I didn't register, I've never paid the full stamp you see, so there's no point. This is where they get away with it isn't it. We ought to register. I realise it now, I don't think enough was known. I don't think we were enlightened enough to know what the benefits were. I realise how stupid I've been. Everybody should pay a full stamp. It's all changed now and this is how it should always have been I think.

In fact, one or two women were prompted by the experience of being unemployed and benefitless to start paying a full National Insurance Contribution: 'It was really to make myself secure again from being made redundant again so I would have something coming in after I'd finished. It seems to have made me think about things like that. I don't think I shall ever feel secure again.' There are still many married women who are not registering because they do not pay a full stamp and therefore do not have any eligibility to unemployment benefit. They are in a sense, the 'leftovers' from the Married Woman's Option.

Married women over 40 do not necessarily benefit from coming back into the National Insurance Scheme. They may not have sufficient working years before retirement to 'earn' for themselves a pension better than the one they would receive on their husband's contributions. (It is younger married women who have really benefited from the 1977 changes.) Knowing they were not entitled to benefit and in the knowledge of high unemployment, many married women simply 'didn't bother' to register: 'I wonder if there's an awful lot like me that didn't register. I didn't because with all this happening I just thought, oh well my age for one thing will go against me, there's so many youngsters unemployed, they're going to take the youngsters before the older people.'

Approximately one-third of the women from Roger Firth did not register as unemployed at any stage of their unemployment. Of those who did register, only a small number registered soon after leaving work, with the rest registering anything from two to three months after redundancy. Although the main reason for non-registration was because they were married women who were not entitled to any unemployment benefit, another important factor in non-registration was the fact that these women had been made redundant. Now because they had been in employment, they had a strong sense of themselves as working women with a claim to work, and consequently such women are more likely to register as unemployed than women who have been out of the labour market for a while. However, this was offset by the fact that everyone received some pay in lieu of notice; ten weeks pay in Harrogate and four weeks in Castleford. This meant that they were not entitled to receive benefit until after this period of notice, and the obvious financial incentive to register was not there. Registration as unemployed really began in earnest as the period of notice expired, but women who found work within this time had often not been registered at all. The real extent of unemployment amongst this group of women was concealed as much by late registration as non-registration, and the unregistered were not only married women but also women who had again 'not bothered' to register as they had been unemployed for only a week or two.

At the time of the research for this book,[6] women could register at their local Job Centres without making a claim for benefit, and so there was no formal barrier to non-registration for anyone. Yet there was a tendency for those women who registered to be the ones who also used the Job Centres and other forms of formal job seeking, whilst unregistered women relied far more on informal methods: 'Well to be truthful I've never been to a Labour Exchange or Job Centre in my life. If I've wanted a job, I've just gone out and got it on my own.' Women do tend to rely on informal methods and local networks to find work (Chaney, 1981) and it is by no means an inferior method. Whilst apparently doing nothing, women had a very comprehensive knowledge of the local labour market, and jobs came *to* them on the local grapevines: 'I didn't go to the Job Centre, or look in the paper or anything. I think when you've been in the trade all your life, there's always connections. If there's anything going you get to know. You get to know of these things by word of mouth sort of thing.'

It has been estimated that as many as half of all unemployed women do not register as such (Market and Opinion Research International (MORI), 1981). The real level of female unemployment is very difficult to know, but the fact that women do not register fuels speculation that in unemployment women are not seriously job seeking. For men registration as unemployed is a much more straightforward affair. It is not any easier: 'It's so degrading, especially at the labour exchange. Not only are they not helpful, they're sometimes hostile and humiliating. Not always, but I had no experience of being unemployed. I didn't know what you're supposed to do. . . .' But for men registration does not have the semblance of personal 'choice'. Unemployed men are required to register as of normal circumstance and they are assumed to be economically active. Most men will qualify for some kind of state benefit, not always on the basis of their National Insurance Contributions, but because men are assumed to be independent wage earners. Conversely, women are assumed to be men's dependants unless they prove otherwise.

Some women did not register, or at least put off registering, because they did not want to be forced to take up a job that they did not really want. It may also be that women are more liable to disqualification. Some women ceased to register after they had been disqualified from benefit for refusing jobs offered to them.

I did register. I started getting unemployment benefit in February – I got about £27. I don't get that now though, I got suspended for refusing two jobs, so they didn't bother, so I haven't bothered with them. They offered me a job at Allerton, well that meant getting two buses which wasn't worth my while, and then they offered me one at Peterfords. Well I didn't want to work there because I've worked with him before, the manager, I didn't like him. I still look in the Job Centre every week though.

On the face of it some women do appear rather choosey, but given women's low wages, the conditions under which they work and their domestic responsibilities, it is easy to see why they might consider a job not worth their while.

Men are also selective about the work they are prepared to do, but men and women seem to restrict their availability for work in different ways. Working women have pressures on their time and are reluctant to work certain hours. They may also limit the distance they are prepared to travel to work, both because of cost and time: 'There was a job in Leeds, in a shop. They were offering £55 a week. It was 8.30 to 5.30 and some nights six o'clock, and that was working Saturdays as well. By the time you'd travelled and paid your bus fare to Leeds, it wouldn't hardly have been worth it.' Men are far more likely to restrict their availability because of the wage offered and the skill needed: 'When I first was

48

made redundant a friend found a job for me at the Magistrates' Court. It was a very respectable "civil service" type job, but the pay was low, £65 a week. I didn't accept it because of that. I never thought I'd end up accepting that kind of wage.' In the end all the men had to come to terms with accepting a lower wage, although they never came to accept anything which approximated to a 'woman's wage' or a 'woman's job', nor would the Job Centre have expected them to. The more skilled men were, the longer they held out to find a job using their skills. All the cutters, for example, were still out of work 12 months after redundancy and knew that they were unlikely to find employment on the basis of those increasingly obsolete skills. Yet they held out: 'It's gone on for too long now. It's demoralising. People ask you if you've got a job yet and what they mean is, "Why haven't you got a job?" I've applied for two cutting jobs. I want a cutting job really.' The point is that men are able to restrict their labour market availability through the male wage and male skills without accruing the same penalties as women's self-imposed restrictions.

Non-registration does not mean that women are not actively job seeking. It is a prerequisite for claiming unemployment benefit and using the full services of the Job Centre. If, however, there is no benefit to be had, or the Job Centres are not perceived as a particularly helpful form of job search, then it is easy to see why women do not register. After all registering as unemployed is not much fun; both men and women find it humiliating. More, to register is to define oneself as one amongst millions, 'on the scrap heap', and that can only be painful.

Men also put off registering if they could. They 'had a holiday first' or 'waited until after Christmas'. Women are faced with a spurious 'choice' and one they should not have, but they do use it to fend off the moment when they have to face the fact that they are redundant and unemployed. Women might try to reconcile themselves to unemployment by strengthening their domestic roots, but unemployment combines an enforced period at home with the process of job seeking. It is impossible to maintain equanimity over the former, whilst actively searching for a job. Whether registered or not, once women start to look for work they define themselves as on the labour market and not at home, and they are no more able to juggle with the irreconcilable facts of unemployment than men.

Local Skills, Local Labour Markets

The conditions of the local labour market are crucial in determining the overall impact of unemployment. The availability of work and the kinds of work available will affect the duration of unemployment, the experience of job search and the terms and conditions of subsequent employment. Although the women from Roger Firth shared the experience of redundancy, their subsequent experience of unemployemnt and being on the labour market diverged. Differences in age and work experience were factors in this, but most importantly they found themselves in quite different local labour market conditions.

One measure of local conditions is the rate of registered unemployment. The higher the rate of inflow on to the unemployment register, the higher the rate of job loss in an area. The rate of unemployment in Castleford is high and this does offer some idea of the extent of closures and redundancies that have occurred around the Castleford area. There are few families that have not been affected by unemployment in some way. However, the duration of unemployment is also a crucial measure of labour market conditions. In Harrogate, for example, a low rate of unemployment combined with a long duration which indicated limited job opportunities. While in Castleford the high rate of unemployment combined with a relatively short duration of unemployment to indicate that job loss is offset to some extent by job creation. More important than the number of job vacancies, is the nature of jobs available. In Harrogate, for example, there was an absolute mismatch between job vacancies and the skills and needs of the former Roger Firth employees.

Harrogate

Harrogate is a small town, 15 miles north of Leeds. It has been, in its day, the Bath of the North of England, a place for the sickly and the wealthy to pass their days. Much of that heritage is still visible and Harrogate is full of large, beautiful houses, expensive shops and luxury hotels. It is a town stamped with middle-class gentility. As Harrogate's popularity as a treatment centre has declined, it has tended to redeploy its resources. Harrogate has more than its fair share of private residential homes for the elderly and has developed as a conference centre and tourist spot for Yorkshire. Unemployment there is below the national average but so is employment. Traditionally it has been a town for retirement, not one in which to work, and in fact many people commute from Harrogate to work in Leeds, Bradford, Ripon and other larger towns nearby. Harrogate does have a small long-established, working-class community and its experience of the town has been one of few jobs and low wages. There is now very little industry in Harrogate. In the period that Roger Firth closed down, ICI and Dunlopillo, the only two large employers in the town, also made many redundant. The service sector is now the main employer with jobs concentrated in shops, hotels, hospitals and residential homes. It is very difficult for men to find work of any kind, and although there tend to be more job opportunities for women, they are mostly confined to low paid, part-time work in cleaning occupations.

The Roger Firth factory had been in operation in Harrogate for over 20 years, making at first rainwear and overcoats, and, later, jackets. The factory workforce was predominantly made up of women who were employed as machinists, operatives and pressers. A small number of men were employed as cutters and pressers. Many of the women from Roger Firth were very skilled clothing workers. They had worked in the industry (sometimes that very factory) for some years and many of them were exceptional for the industry now, in being able to 'make through' a garment. They often referred to themselves as 'tailoresses' rather than machinists. Although in recent years more and more younger women had been taken on, at the time of the redundancy the Harrogate workforce was made up predominantly of very skilled women in their forties.

The factory was a very stable and close working environment, indicative of the lack of alternative employment opportunities in the area, as much as anything. Roger Firth rarely had to recruit labour on the open market. Once employed there, people tended to draw in members of their families, so that the labour force was actually a network of mothers and daughters, fathers and sons, uncles, cousins and siblings; it was also the making of many marriages. When people said that the factory was like 'family' there was some measure of truth in that, as well as indicating their attachment to the factory:

> I enjoyed every minute, 'cause all my friends were on that section. We used to have a right laugh and joke and I miss them all now. We could chat when we were working, that's what I liked.

> I don't think I've really got over it yet, because you're missing something. There's one chap, he said to me – we seemed to talk more in those last few weeks – 'You know it's pretty rotten when you've worked all your life with the same people, you see them more than you see your own family, and then it's all gone.'

They could not expect to find that kind of working environment and the connections again, for, as it turned out, the local labour market offered virtually no opportunity to find comparable work in clothing, nor the pay and conditions.

Castleford

Castleford is a working-class mining town in West Yorkshire, physically and culturally dominated by coal pits. The National Coal Board is the main employer in the area and husbands, fathers and boyfriends of the women from Roger Firth were, in fact, mostly National Coal Board employees. There is now very little other work for men. Employment for women in the area started to expand in the 1970s when numerous clothing factories and one large sweet factory moved into Castleford, drawing upon the labour of miners' wives. The recession has affected Castleford as elsewhere. Pits have closed down and the local sweet factory closed down its twilight shift – the only significant opportunity for part-time work in Castleford – laying off hundreds of women. The rate of unemployment in Castleford for both men and women has increased steadily from 1979.

The factory at Castleford made men's trousers and had been operating for 11 years. With the exception of the manager, the workforce was entirely women, predominantly in their early twenties. Unlike the Harrogate factory, Castleford was highly rationalised and very efficient and the machinists' skills were more limited to a narrow range of operations. At one time the factory had a high labour turnover as women moved from factory to factory to improve their wage conditions. By the late 1970s this began to change as the number of job vacancies in clothing sharply contracted. In the last few years of its existence the Castleford factory also had a very stable labour force. Although Castleford had nothing like the 'history' of the Harrogate Roger Firth, it too was an extremely tight-knit factory. The factory/family connection was just as dominant and, as well as being mothers and daughters, sisters, cousins, aunts and nieces, many of the women had gone to school and grown up together. The 'girls' were the bonus of factory life: 'We all got on like a family you know. I think it was the best factory ever. Everyone was so close together and we all got on. I was just happy at Roger Firth. We had a right good set of girls, everybody together, there was a unity.'

Both sets of women leaving Roger Firth shared the experience of having enjoyed relatively well-paid work under good employment conditions. They shared an experience of the same industry and offered broadly similar skills on the job market. The difference was that while there were still job opportunities for women in the clothing industry in Castleford (although very little indeed outside of that), in Harrogate there was no work available in clothing and the women's skills died with the jobs.

Closing Options (1)

In Harrogate there was virtually no opportunity for the women from Roger Firth to find new jobs in the clothing industry and this made a substantial impact on their subsequent experience of unemployment. It took them a long time to find work. The average period of unemployment was 6 months and a few women were still out of work 18 months after the factory closure. Their age did not help, some of them were in their fifties and, as they quickly discovered, in a contracting labour market employers preferred young people:

> There's so many youngsters unemployed these days, and they're going to take them on before the older people. The thing is there's such a terrific response to all the jobs. In the old days, they would get two or three replies, now they'll get a hundred.

> Wherever you go now, they ask your age and most of them want younger ones, and those that do want older women, well there's about 60 or 70 of us after it. They're wanting to take teenagers on because it's cheaper for them, naturally.

> I applied for a job at the new supermarket and I've worked in a supermarket before. With my husband being in the Air Force, I've taken what's going and I've lots of experience. But it doesn't matter what experience you've had, they're all young girls that they've taken on.

It was entirely older women who made up the long-term unemployed in Harrogate, but age was only part of the problem.
The real problem was that they were *deskilled* by the labour market. They had been skilled machinists but, since there were no local job opportunities for clothing machinists, they were effectively on the labour market as unskilled labour. As unskilled labour, they joined the many, chasing few jobs:

> Have you been in there? [unemployment office] It puts you off – queues of them. Then the people who work there, they never

seem to rush. You feel like saying, 'Come on, hurry up!'

I'm sick of looking in the Job Centre. Every time I go in there – they must think I'm crazy, I pore over every single one. I get the local paper but there's very, very few jobs.

What jobs did exist were mostly cleaning jobs which they regarded with differing degrees of enthusiasm.

I knew I could always find something. I knew that if the worst came to the worst, I could always go and clean for somebody, not that I like it, but I knew that I could do something if I was desperate for money.

It suits me fine. I'd said I'd never take a cleaning job but when you think about it, you're cleaning and polishing at home aren't you?

The only thing I will not take is cleaning, no way. I hate doing it anyway.

They all chased after the same jobs, whatever they were:

You get to hear about jobs through the local grapevine; girls have been after jobs, or they've heard of a job and we all make a dive down there. We all went over to Ripon the other day to a chicken factory. The chickens were put on to racks and tied up by their legs and the feathers plucked out of them. Another job you actually had to put your hand right inside. Ugh! I thought, 'Oh no!' And it stank that place. One woman took a job there, she said she'd take it because she had a mortgage and no husband. Then we all went over to Sports Fashions, a non-union place. He asked us what we'd been earning and we told him and he said, 'Well you won't get that here.' They didn't even have a canteen. He said he'd got a room where we could make tea but we had to bring our own stuff so that meant carting tea, sugar and milk and your sandwiches every day. And you know what it's like when you get up in the morning. Especially for married women anyway. You get up, you get the kids their breakfast and men are worse than the kids . . . by the time you come to get your own sandwiches, well you can forget it. Roger Firth had a super canteen. You could always buy toast and tea in the morning and they always put on a good meal at lunch time. Anyway I didn't get that job either. If you've had anything to do with unions they don't want to know you.

And the longer it went on, the more demoralising and desperate it became: 'I went along for this interview and I got myself dressed up and everything and the interview was amazing. He said he'd about 20 more people to see and he said I'd be surprised at the people he'd interviewed, the stories they've told, they're desperate for jobs. And I just sat there and I thought, "Well I'm desperate, I need a job." ' The only way these women, of *all* ages, were to find work was by being extremely flexible. *Flexibility* was the keystone to finding work in Harrogate.

Women found work in shops, hotels, hospitals, old people's homes, the Army camp and even sometimes in private houses. They became shop assistants, nursing auxillaries, cooks and cleaners; mostly cleaners.

I'm an auxillary nurse at a private old people's home. I do everything, there are no SRN's, you are the nurse. There's a cook and a cleaner but if I'm not busy then I help in the kitchen. I work from eight o'clock till two o'clock. I have to work alternate weekends – he's [husband] not too keen on that. Fortunately I don't mind wiping bottoms. It's not very pleasant but for some people there's no way they'd do it, but I don't mind really.

It took me nearly three months to find a job. I'm a chambermaid. We start at 8 and finish at 4.30 and our gross pay is £54 and by the time they take off tax and that I come home with about £45, and by the time I've paid my Mum, I've nothing left for myself. I come home from work and I'm tired out. I come home and I'm flaked out.

I'm working now, part time but I'm working. I was out of work all that time. It's cleaning, well it's contract cleaning up at the Army camp. They put an advert in the paper and I just rang up and I got it without an interview. I'm just cleaning the billets out.

I'm a domestic out at the psychiatric hospital. It's a job, I like it, but it isn't my job is it? It isn't sewing.

Women were not only flexible in terms of the jobs and work they were prepared to do, but also in terms of the conditions of work, pay and hours. At Roger Firth they had been mostly full-time workers (even part-timers had usually worked a 30-hour week) on a full-time wage working fixed, weekday hours. The vast majority ended up not only in a totally different occupation, and invariably on a reduced wage, but also working shift hours and part-time hours. Although most women were pleased to have a job of any kind, the hours of work caused them the most problems. Full-time work invariably meant shift work causing havoc with domestic order: 'I'm a domestic. I work 40 hours a week. One week it's 7 until 4, with an hour for lunch, and the next it's 11 until 8. Every other week I have Saturday and Sunday off. The other week I have Tuesday and Wednesday. My husband isn't too keen. He doesn't like me working weekends. It just doesn't fit in and it never will.' Or, and most usually, they were trapped in part-time work.

Part-time work for women is assumed to be organised around women's needs for flexibility, to be able to combine their paid work with their domestic responsibility. Now whilst part-time work may be offered as a 'concession' to attract women, it is clear that is not the reason for its proliferation, especially in recession. One woman's account of her new job indicates how her cleaning work had been reorganised and transformed, from full-time hours to part-time hours, to increase efficiency and reduce costs. Her part-time, shift hours included a split working day. It is clear that it is not part-time work that is flexible, but women:

I do 9.30 to 11.30 and then 2 to 4.30 every other day. It's quite good money, £1.59 an hour. They bring you home, so you're in town by 11.45, so I do my shopping and they pick you up again at 1.40. They used to be on government contract work out there, employed by the army, but it was costing too much, so they brought in a private contractor. They're trying to edge all of them (full-timers) out and put everybody on the same as what we're doing. It's great, the hours suit me fine. I do Saturdays and Sundays, it makes your money up, they pay you time and a half. Last week I had Friday off then I worked Saturday morning, had a break for a couple of hours at Saturday dinner time. I went and did all my shopping and brought it home, had a quick bite and then was back off again at 1.40. I got home about quarter to five and just came straight in and prepared the tea for them. I got all my vegetables ready and cooked my meat, on Saturday, ready for Sunday, so that all I had to do when I walked in on Sunday dinner time was to put the gas on. I do 20 hours a week and it's £1.59 an hour but with getting extra for doing the weekends, it's quite good money.

With a two-and-a-half hour, unpaid break in the middle of the day such working hours are not convenient at all, but because working unsocial hours can boost low rates of pay, and because she can squeeze the shopping in between her split shift, it 'suits' her. She and the shopping are flexible. It can be done as well on Saturday lunch-time as on Friday night. Here the sexual division of labour makes some sense of her working hours.

This is not always the case. One woman who was absolutely dependent on her own wage, a full-time wage, was forced into taking two part-time jobs in order to earn something that approximated to a living wage. Even then, two part-time wages turned out less than one full-time wage:

I started in February at the old folks' 'hotel', that was a part-time job and I came out with about £29. I was also working in a pub for four nights a week and I was coming out with £13 there. It was very tight. But then in July, I started at the General Hospital. I'm a domestic, the money's very good. Before tax it's about £85, and I still do the pub job. It's a lot better now although I don't really like it. Well the actual work itself is alright. You can't really complain, apart from working weekends. I get one off in every three. It's hard work, physical work and you're completely on the go from the minute you come in to the minute you leave.

In another instance, a part-time job was combined with private enterprise:

When I first left Roger Firth I started this cleaning job three mornings a week. She was very nice and the job was alright but it just wasn't me. I don't know, I have enough of my own cleaning without doing someone else's. Then I got this job at the school and I finished with her a week before. It's doing the school meals. I work there from 11.30 to 1.30 five days a week. It works out at about £15.20 I think. I had it on the understanding that it's from term to term. Well they gave me a retainer, half pay, which they weren't going to give me. But at the same time they said that if I decided I didn't wish to take this post, I had to give them a fortnight's notice, which was silly really, because they said if the numbers weren't right they wouldn't be employing me. I've started my own business as well. I started that about the same time. I'm selling pots – pottery, I sell them at parties mostly. It does get a bit complicated. I've either got to get a babysitter or take her with me. If it's a church do and that starts at 8 o'clock, then I can be away by 9.30 and I take her with me, but if it's a house do, I like to leave her at home with a babysitter because we most likely sit around drinking coffee and talking and it gets a bit drawn out.

When it becomes apparent that women are taking two part-time jobs in order to earn anything like enough money to meet their needs, then the idea that part-time work is organised to suit women's convenience, becomes a ludicrous one. Part-time work cheapens women's labour, and because it is not so well protected as full-time work, the conditions of such employment often come to resemble casual work. An even more stark form of this casualisation is homework, which one or two women from Harrogate did end up doing. The local papers regularly carried advertisements for homeworkers but the majority of women did not consider it worth their while despite their difficulties in finding work. They were at least *able* to go out to work, whereas it does seem that the women most likely to take up homework are those confined to the home for one reason or another. (Hope *et al.*, 1976.) Most women would not consider homework because it was so exploitative:

> I've taken sewing in at home in the past, but I wouldn't do it now though. I went after one lot, it was scatter cushions, but you'd have been up all night to get those numbers done. He wanted thousands doing for a bit of a wage, and the wage wouldn't have done me a bit of good because of the extra electricity. It would have taken me all my time to pay the electric bill. So I said no thanks. I think he's still advertising and always will at those rates.

But in fact there is always somebody who is pleased to do it: 'I work on my own machine, so you're using your own electricity but I'd rather do it than nothing. I don't think I will get a job unless I get a cleaning job. It's never more than a £1 an hour, but I can work my own hours. I do feel isolated as regards not seeing my friends and that.' As much as anything else it is occupying:

> I suppose you could term it soft furnishings, making cushion covers, napkins and table cloths, all sorts of things like that. It was advertised in the paper but I actually went into where they were and they said yes they were willing to take me on. They'd had hundreds of applications so it was perhaps the personal touch, me going out there. I said to my husband, well I've nothing to lose. I may as well keep occupied and see how it goes.

It was homework which provided the only outlet for these women's skills: 'You look back and think, it's just a waste. I mean

Mr Holt rang me up once and he was asking me what the girls were doing. I mean there's one girl in a lottery box in town and things like that, and he said, you could tell he was full up, "What an absolute waste of good girls," and that's really what it is. None of them have gone back into clothing, not because they don't want to. There just aren't any jobs.'

Closing Options (2)

Castleford, on the other hand, is a two job town:

> It is not very good. You see the main industry here has been textiles and mining and now that they're taking the textiles away I don't think there are many opportunities for women. I think it's better for a man because you see it's a mining village and there are lots of jobs for men, but for women I'd say it's not very good at the moment. It's more a man's world round here.

> There's nothing really apart from clothing. There's quite a few pits around but there's nothing else really. It's got to be quite a black spot has Castleford on work.

On the face of it, the women from Castleford fared better. The majority of women had found work within four weeks and some had found alternative work before they had even left Roger Firth. Even older women found jobs, although it took a little longer, and 12 months after redundancy all the women who had been job seeking were back in work. With the exception of *one* woman, they all went back into clothing. Once other local manufacturers got wind of the closures they came to the factory to recruit labour. In Castleford, trained machinists are still wanted, even in recession. Indeed, the clothing industry continues to offer employment *precisely* because of the unstable economic conditions. In a perverse and short-term way, it maintains its operations. As one firm closes down, another moves in mopping up redundant labour and even sometimes occupying the same factory site. Recession has created very difficult trading conditions for the industry, yet provides ideal conditions for the supply of a cheap, skilled, labour force. It is still the case that small firms can be more competitive and resilient than larger ones and still new producers are tempted to try their hand.

The relatively short period of unemployment in Castleford was due entirely to the clothing industry's ability to reabsorb the women from Roger Firth, even if as in one woman's case, it was not as a machinist.

We were told that Peterfords were setting on employees from Roger Firth. They only wanted Roger Firth girls because they knew what they were like. We did have a good reputation and so they were setting some on. But by the time I got back [after a break for Christmas] they'd seen everybody and filled all the positions. I went to the Job Centre anyway and said were they still taking any on there and she said they were all filled, but I thought I'd give it a go anyway, so I went down there on my own bat and I just went to see the personnel manager, just to see if there was anything going. This is where my luck came in. The woman who's the personnel manageress, she also does the family planning so I knew her by sight. Anyway I was telling her I needed a job and she said, how desperate are you and I said, well, desperate. She said there wasn't anywhere in the factory but they did want someone in the canteen. So I took it.

Their new conditions of work were not as good. Some women ended up working in neighbouring towns: Pontefract, Knottingly, Featherstone, even Leeds and Tadcaster. Although not great distances, they added time to an already finely-balanced day, and costs from a not over-large wage packet. In a contracted job market women can't be too choosy whilst employers can:

I was in the Job Centre and there was this girl from Roger Firth and she was trying at this place because it was near her home. When she enquired about it they wanted to know what experience she had. And she said she could do all the way round trousers – she could make trousers – and they asked her if she could do anything on jackets and she couldn't. So they said she'd be no good, they wanted someone who had experience on how to make jackets besides trousers.

Quite contrary to the Harrogate experience, women from Castleford had no real opportunity for either part-time work or work outside of clothing. The labour market was absolutely inflexible. This was illustrated by one woman who, at the age of 39, married, with no children, decided that the redundancy was the opportunity for change. She wanted part-time work, but 18 months after redundancy, she was still looking: 'I'm never bored but I miss the money. There's not a lot going and you see everyone's after part-time jobs. I mean I've done my whack. I've worked 25 years, but if something came up, part-time, I'd definitely take it. If Roger Firth hadn't closed down I'm sure I'd still have been there. I liked it there, it was a lovely place. I'd have been pensioned off.'

Castleford has never offered women a wide range of employment opportunities, but in recession that has become severely restricted. However, the conditions of recession have not only limited women's choices and allowed employers to recruit from a larger pool of labour, but in the clothing industry it has also made possible an intensification of work under increasingly exploitative conditions. (See Chapter 1 for a fuller discussion.) In one local factory wages have been held down by the simple expedient of the threat of closure: 'I mean they've got no rise at all this year, not a penny, so therefore those girls are working for less money. The union got 5 percent but they won't pay it. They told them if they don't get 5,000 trousers out a week as from now, they'll shut it.' Now pay has been combined with impossible work speeds that even the most experienced machinist cannot achieve.

They were advertising in the paper, so I thought I would go and see. It was a nice little place, but in fact when I went down, this woman who was sat in front of me, said there'd been four on that job and they'd all left and I didn't know why, but I did after a bit! I had to do sleeve making and collar making. I had 17 sleeves to do and 45 collars in an hour. Well I could do the sleeves but I couldn't do the collars with it!

Whilst it was the case that all the women from Castleford Roger Firth had found alternative work within a 12-month period, many women *left* those jobs, either voluntarily because of worsening conditions or because they had been made redundant again. Nearly one-third of the women had a second spell out of work within an 18-month period. There was another pregnancy. So although the women fared quite well in terms of the speed with which they found work, they were confined to the single unstable industry with poor conditions and now with little or no employment protection rights. If the condition of the clothing industry deteriorates further, the position of women employed within it will be very bleak indeed: 'There's a lot of girls employed in the clothing trade now, who wouldn't attempt to go into clothing if they had any choice. You could talk to any of the girls and they'd say if they could get another job, they wouldn't stay there. Between you and me I've always said sewing was slave labour.'

The Real Meaning of Unemployment

A period of unemployment often creates a weaker employment situation and other redundancy studies have shown how both men and women will be forced to accept less favourable conditions of employment with lower pay and less skilled work (Daniel and Stilgoe, 1977). But now women are even more restricted and their working conditions ever worsening. Although the labour market conditions in Castleford and Harrogate turned out to be absolutely different in terms of the employment opportunities open to women, they both illustrate the *inflexibility* of the labour market. They illustrate differently the same phenomena: the exploitation of female labour. In the space of two years the women of Roger Firth have moved from being skilled clothing workers with relatively good pay and conditions, job protection and trade union organisation, to occupying low-paid, insecure work, with non-unionisation often a condition of employment. They perceive clearly enough what is happening to them as women: 'Women can get jobs if they're willing to do dirty jobs, like cleaning. Men won't do that, that's a woman's job. Men won't work for that pay.' And as working-class women:

> If you want a job you have to take less money and that's it, or be prepared to take a job other than that what you've trained to do. That's what they're doing you see, they can take people on for less money now, get people for less. It's pushed the wages right down.

> I don't think any of the closures are necessary. They say it's the workers that want more money, but it's not the workers. I had an argument with a director once. I was a passer and bad work had gone out. He sat there and was comparing us with Germans and how efficient they were, and I sat until I couldn't stand it any longer. I said, don't you blame the people on the shop floor, you're the people who are to blame. You are the people who make the decisions on how many these factories should turn out. I said, 'When I first came here you wanted 2,000 pairs of trousers a week, then you wanted 2,500, then you wanted 3,000. But you don't modernise the machinery, all you do is expect us to work that much harder, it's your British directorship!' It's not just textiles, it's being done throughout industry. They're investing abroad where there's cheap labour and they're keeping us down as far as they can. It's not just that you're years on the dole, even those who've got jobs, they've taken large wage cuts. If you get another job you have to accept less money. I think it's all done to bring our standard of living down. I do think it's Margaret Thatcher's idea with all this unemployment to bring wages down.

What is less clear is how to fight back.

4
Five Women

The following chapter is comprised of five women's accounts of how redundancy affected and interrupted their lives. Personal circumstances at the time of redundancy are clearly a crucial factor in determining how job loss is experienced. One woman, for example, had a baby, and so although her life has been transformed, those changes are primarily connected with mother-hood rather than redundancy. For another woman the redundancy coincided with the break-up of her marriage, and for her the experiences of isolation and financial hardship arose from both events. Yet, despite these very individually-experienced situations, there are shared themes running through the accounts and indeed through this book. These women talk about the inadequacy of the male wage as a sole source of income and this is especially highlighted by the now common occurrence of their men being out of work. They show how they felt the loss of their own wage, not just as the loss of income, but as a loss of independence. They demonstrate how the combination of paid work and unpaid work in the home can only be achieved by an exhausting 'routine' in which men do *not* participate. Above all, they indicate how work is axiomatic to their lives and redundancy does not present itself as an occasion to return to the home. Even the two women who are not in work understand it as a temporary position; until the children go to school or the job market picks up. Rather, redundancy is an interruption of women's *working* lives.

Susan Peters:

I was a back seamer at Roger Firth, that's the back seam of a pair of trousers. I'd measure them up and sew the seam down. I was also shop steward. I started in the clothing industry before I was married but that was in Leeds and I found it a long way to travel and so I started to work in shops. I worked in a man's shop and a draper's shop so really I'm quite experienced for quite a few jobs. I've always worked, I've never stopped working and I don't think I could. I can't stay at home all the time, because I'm not a visitor you see. I can't go round talking to people, not even family. If I'm at home I get really bored. When my girls were small I used to work on a night time. I waited until they were about six months and then I worked at night, in the fish shop next door actually. I worked there until they were old enough to go to school. I never left them until then. Once they were at school I went back to full-time work. They're good girls, they've never caused me a minute's trouble, they've been healthy, they haven't had much illness and my husband has always worked regular days. He's home by 1.45 so he's been at home when they've come home from school. They've never been neglected. I've never had to leave them with anybody.

Then when they went to school I managed a general store, it sold everything, and I did that for four years. Then my father got ill and because I was the only daughter I had to look after him. After he died, I had a sort of nervous breakdown and I didn't work for nine months. Then a friend told me about a job going at Roger Firth and I went down and asked about it. I was there for over five years. I was happy there. I think everybody gets fed up with work some time or the other, especially a woman, the pressures of home, you think you'd like to stay at home, but I always feel it changed my life that job at Roger Firth. I wouldn't say boo to a goose when I first went there. By gum it brought me out and now I'll always stand up for myself. I think it was the women. It was an upsetting experience when Firth's closed. You never think you're going to be made redundant.

There was only one person in our household who was made redundant and it was only a matter of months before I got a job, but in some households there's two or three people out of work and that must be terrible. I've been married 17 years and so we had our home and everything. We just had to live, which we could do on my husband's wage. I've not been one for debts. I've always been careful that we should try and live on one wage. When I got made redundant it really made me think. We managed alright because we weren't buying a house then, but I thought well you come to lose £50 or £60 a week coming in and it's a lot of money if you've got commitments for that money. I don't think I shall ever feel secure again.

I registered with the Job Centre straight away, well after Christmas. I didn't get any dole money at all because at the time I was only paying a married woman's stamp, but now I've been paying a full stamp. It's making myself secure from being made redundant again really, so I would have something coming in after I'd finished. Something's better than nothing isn't it? It seems to have made me think about things like that. I missed having my own money. It made me feel guilty about buying anything. Really I got a bit low that way because things that normally I would have bought, I couldn't because I wasn't earning a wage. Or if I did, I felt guilty. You definitely lose your independence. I suppose it depends on the standard of living you want, but when you've got a family, you need two wages.

It's not been as difficult for me as it has been for some of the other girls, because I've done other jobs, but I've had a lot of interviews for a lot of jobs. There's nothing much going in this area apart from tailoring and one or two shops. There's a sweet factory but that's on the brink of shutting. I was out of work for about two months and then I went to Peterford's. I worked there for about five weeks. I left because I couldn't stand it. You see at Roger Firth it was piece-work, but at least you fetched your own work and you pushed it away when you'd finished with it, so you got that break. Whereas at Peterford's you went in on a morning, you sat on a chair in front of your machine, they fetched your work to you at your side, and they took it away from you, so you never moved. They hadn't had a rise for three years and things like that. So they started to talk among the others and they asked me to become union representative and I didn't want it. It made it a bit difficult for me really, I think that's maybe why I left.

I didn't have another job to go to. I'm having a little bit of trouble with my nerves. I think once you've had trouble with nerves it comes back. I wasn't too good really so I had a couple of months at home again. I must admit I quite enjoyed those few months off. It was summer and I lay out in the back garden all afternoon. I think better of myself for not working all hours and trying to fit things in, but in my mind I was worse off, worried because I was trying to stretch the money further. The summer months weren't too bad because I was gardening but these winter months if I'm in the house, I feel a bit shut in. I'm glad to see the end of this year, it's not been a good year for me. I was very settled at Roger Firth, you get up in the morning, you go to work, you come home, you know what's going to happen, you get into a sort of routine. I've thought about it a lot. I didn't like being without a job because I've always had a job. I can't really say I'm a housewife, because that isn't what you're doing for a job is it? Well, it's a job, but it's not a paid job as such.

Whether it was the effect of the redundancy I don't know, but I decided not to go back into tailoring at all. I enjoy sewing but I have lost faith in the industry I think. So I found a shop job, as checkout operator in Asda. It was part-time, five afternoons a week and I got about £34 a week. I was getting about £55 at Firth's. Anything was better than nothing but I'd have preferred full-time work. Two teenage daughters take a lot of keeping. Well after working as a part-time checkout operator they just asked me if I wanted to be a supervisor, full time, I've been doing it for about a month now. I'm the supervisor of the checkouts. There's about 24 girls doing different shifts, some afternoons, some just weekends, it's spread out, so that the tills have always got someone on them, they're never vacant. I work out the shift rota, their hours and their wages. It's lovely. They're nice girls and I enjoy working with them. It took a while really for me to settle down because I liked the girls at Roger Firth and I didn't seem to be able to find a situation like that again, until now. It's a well-paid job, although there are hours that you don't get paid for. I get nearly £80 a week, I bring home about £56 after tax and everything. I have a full day off in the week and half a day and Sunday as well. They're lovely to work for, and they look after their staff. There's just one thing that I'm not keen on and that's the late nights. I have to work one late night a week and I'm there before eight o'clock in the morning and it's 8.15 at night before I get out. It's very tiring and I have to do that once a week. I get one weekend off in three – it's better than most shop jobs.

It came at a good time really because we've had a bad patch this year, with money. My husband was off four months from work with his back. He's never been off sick with anything before and it was terrible because we didn't know what sick money was or how to deal with it, so it was a good job I had a job because we didn't get any help from anywhere. We had just taken on this house over ten years so it is a big amount to pay every month and the bills just rolled in, water rates, ordinary rates, electric. . . . The Coal Board did give him make-up pay but it only worked out that he was getting £50 odd a week, which is not a lot. I mean on Friday night I spend £37 or thereabouts on what I call my big shop, just on Friday nights. It goes nowhere does it? My redundancy money – it was about £1,000 altogether – has all gone! It went towards buying this house and some went towards our holiday. I manage the money really because my husband is not a very good saver, and he's quite happy with that. His money gets paid into the bank and we have our mortgage and things paid out of that. For food we just draw so much out and he has so much for the car and that and whatever's left we put into the building society, it works like that. I go out to work to provide for clothes, the car, holidays and things like that. We just couldn't do it if I didn't work.

I get tired but I try and organise myself. When I was at Firth's, I used to do the shopping on Friday night after work and then Saturday and Sunday I used to get really stuck in. I used to wash on Sunday, I used to prepare my meals the night before and just leave instructions for my eldest daughter, she's very helpful. My husband's not bad but he's not very domesticated. He'll wash up and things like that but he can't cook and he wouldn't clean, but he's very handy around the house, he's just built me that kitchen extension. Then with part-time work, I had my mornings at home to do a few jobs. I'd cook a meal in the mornings, stew or anything.

I'd do it in the pressure cooker, prepare all the vegetables and get things done so it's all ready you see when I came home. I've always been like that because it does save time. You just have to do things when you've got time. But now as far as the routine of the house is concerned, I haven't really got back into the swing of full-time work yet. I haven't got a routine at all. I keep trying and I think well it's my day off tomorrow and I'll do so and so, then I'll get some visitors, or something happens, or I have to go somewhere. I cook a meal every night. I have to because the girls only take a packed lunch to school, they won't have school dinners and I have my brother now. He's just getting divorced and so he comes here for his meals as well. So I have to cook a meal of a night and by the time you've cleared away, washed up and that, your night's nearly over. I think with full time you learn to keep going. I sort of think if I sit down, I won't get up again, so I try and do what I can before I sit down. But I find it tiring. I think it's being on a part-time basis for those months and I'd really started to enjoy it in some ways, having half a day at home and half a day at work, and I could do what I liked in the evenings.

I wouldn't ask my husband to do anything in the house because I know he wouldn't be able to do it really – he'd try because he's good really but I don't want to put too much on him. My eldest daughter is very good, she's terrific really. I've only got to say, 'I could do with doing this' and she'll say, 'I'll do it Mum'. I don't know how I'd manage without her. Mind you when you've got children in the house, it's not the same as having two adults. You've got so much more to clear up after. Really I suppose I work full time mainly for them. I want them to do well at school. What I really want is for them not to have to depend on anybody. I want them to get a good education, something at the back of them, so that they can look after themselves, they don't need anybody. I think it goes back . . . I was only 16 when I lost my mother and I was the only girl, I had three brothers and I had the housework and a job to do then. When I got married I had my own house and my father's house. It's something that I don't want my daughters to have. I didn't have anybody to push me with my education and that's why I think I've done it with my two girls and I've been lucky because they're both very, very clever, both of them, I'm so proud of them. I've always made a lot of them with school. I've always been interested in their work, I've always gone to every open night and that. I just want to make them settled and they can be self-sufficient if need be. I suppose that's my life.

Phyllis Collins:

I was a machinist at Roger Firth, making up linings. It was part time but it wasn't far off full-time. I used to work from 8.30 to 4.40. I think I used to bring about £35 to £40 home. It worked out to just over £1 an hour. I started there 12 years ago when we moved from Keighley. I didn't know anyone here and I got really depressed. My little lad wasn't more than two. I had worked in Keighley – they used to have an evening shift – and I thought I'm going to ring this Roger Firth up to see if they've got an evening shift. Anyway I did and they said they were sorry but it took them all their time to fill the machines during the day never mind about an evening shift, but he said if ever I could get through the day to go and see him. Anyway my nerves got worse. I think it was being cooped up and not knowing anybody. I enquired about putting Roger in a nursery and I got him in one that took him at three. So I rang up again and I got the job. I lived on Maple Avenue then. It was walking distance to the bus station on the Leeds Road and I used to pass the nursery on the way, so it was quite handy. He loved it too. I think it did him good because he wasn't any trouble going to school. Then after work I'd just get off the bus, pick him up and walk home. I was there ever since.

We were all upset when it closed, it took a while to sink in. To be quite honest I kept thinking that they'd send for us again. I didn't register as unemployed. I didn't pay the full stamp. It's just something you don't usually do when you're working and you've got kids. They didn't seem to accept it from married women anyway, because you're always on and off when your kiddies are little, there's always something the matter. I wish I'd paid it now, but you don't realise at the time, that little bit coming in would have been better than nothing. I've tried for certain jobs as I've seen them in the paper. I didn't look at first. I thought I'd have a little time at home and my daughter was getting married. I've tried once or twice at the hospital where my friend Mary is working. I've tried for a machinist job although I didn't really want sewing. I've never been in the Job Centre. I suppose I'll have to try in there but my friends go in there and some have got jobs and some haven't. I look through the papers. There are one or two who keep their ears and eyes open for me. If a sewing job came up, I'd take it for the sake of having a job. I'd like to work over at the hospital, though, it's only over at the back of us. Now with bus fares, it's a bit ridiculous going too far. It was costly enough when I was at Roger Firth. It depends on your wage, if you're not getting a lot it's not worth paying a lot out in bus fares. I'd like a job close to my own home. It's not just the cost. Time adds on to your working hours. If you don't finish work until 4.45 and you've half an hour bus ride, it's going to be six o'clock by the time you get home. I think it gets more desperate to look as time gets on. The first few months were like a holiday. I never thought to look. I think I feel it a bit more because we had a wedding in August and it took the money that we had. I feel now that I need a job more than ever to try and get back on our feet.

It's difficult on one wage, you've just not as much money to go round have you? We never go out. We didn't go out much before. We like country music, both of us and if there were groups on at a club or anything, that's when we went out. We did go out on Saturday to see Andy Williams at Scarborough and that was a real treat because we haven't been out for months. I felt guilty though because I felt we shouldn't be going. I think it's a bit harder living in general but I do miss not being able to afford to go out if you want. I have to make do now a lot more, and probably a lot more as we go on, if things don't get better. It makes you wonder how far it can all go. If it had happened a few years back, it would have been a lot harder, there were four of them to feed then, but now my eldest son lives away, and my two girls are married. I've still got Peter at home. He'd like to have gone in the Navy, but he can't get in so he's going on to further education. It would have been better if he'd got into the Navy. My husband works during the week at the further education college, but on Sundays he has this other job at the hospital. He's a chef, well actually he's a baker by trade, but he's a chef as well. He gets paid into the bank every month, just over £300 a month and he gets £12 for Sundays. I used to use my wage packet first. I never kept any money for myself, it all went into the house. Now when I was working it was easy, but since I finished work we aren't getting that extra money coming in. Some of my redundancy went on my daughter's wedding, the rest has just gone on living. I used to try and put something away each month out of his wages, but I couldn't.

I'm doing this bit of soldering now. I wouldn't call it work. Last week it brought in about £12 I think. It has all come about by accident. It's my daughter's work actually, she was doing it and not getting it all through. She works full time and she was doing this at home in the evenings. They were waiting for her and she asked me if I wanted some to do. I said yes, I would help. It's nothing guaranteed. They might not want anymore after today. I didn't think it would last as long as this. I thought I would have to get a job after Christmas, but anyway he's kept ringing up. I'm doing plugs right now. Like all homework you have to do about 200 to earn £1.25. I don't do a right lot, because as I say it takes quite a long time to do not many if you know what I mean. The most I ever earn is about £15 a week. It just helps with the weekend groceries. It depends on how many I do, and how many they want. I'd say I do about four hours a day. Sometimes actually, in the evenings, if I'm on my own, I knock up a few for morning. You see when you're working at home you can do that, you can do it when you want. I don't class it as a job actually, not for the bit that I earn, so I just say, I'm just at home, I don't work. Actually I was speaking to my sister-in-law only this weekend, she'd rung up and she said, 'Are you still not working?' and I automatically said, 'No'. But I don't tell folk about it, very few, because I don't class it as a job. If I was earning £20 or £30 I would, but some weeks it's only £10.

I wouldn't get a proper job doing this. They're all young girls and they don't pay a right lot. My daughter doesn't like it. It's a case that she sticks it because there is nothing much else to do. It would be no good me trying to get a job down there. I don't enjoy doing it, but to be honest I haven't tried for anything for ages and this [homework] might be one of the reasons. But I keep thinking things will pick up, so I'd wait a bit, which I still think they probably will in time. There seem to be a few more jobs around than there used to be. Sometimes I'll say I'll have to really start looking again. I must seem right lazy, but I've always worked, even when the kiddies were little, so I'm not lazy – I'll say it's my age. Mind you, in the winter, when all the snow comes and the rain, I'd sit and I used to look out and I'd think thank goodness I haven't got to go out. Now even in the summer when it comes right nice, I'm able to go and sit outside.

I've got more time now. I get up and get Roger off to school. He goes for about eight o'clock and then I sit and have my cup of tea and a bit of breakfast. If I do it as I should do, I get this [homework] out of the way early so I can finish after dinner time and then just tidy up. I might watch a film on TV or sit with my knitting. Nearer tea time, I have to start and do the tea. My son comes home at about 4.20 and my husband will be in about six o'clock. Usually I have tea ready for five o'clock and then keep his [husband's] warm until he's home. Otherwise Peter's starving. He's right lanky, like a bean pole and he's always starving. On Wednesday, my husband works late, it's his night for the evening class, so we don't wait for him and me and Roger have our tea early. I used to clean and that when I came in from work and at weekends. My husband used to do a bit but he never bothered really and it doesn't worry him now! I used to do my washing mainly Sunday mornings because he goes to work then. Now I do it all as I come to it. I do it when I'm ready.

Being out of work, I think it gets worse as you go on. I think you lose your confidence. I find that. When I see something in the paper I dread having to go. I'm alright when I get there, but I go through terrible things while I'm going. I really felt sick having to go for that last job, but once I sat down and was talking to him, I was alright. I just think it's confidence and I'm not one for changes anyway. I just like to plod on in my own way. The longer you're out of work the less confidence you've got for going and trying. I think we all need to work. I like to work. I'd prefer to go out to work than be at home, even if it's only part time. I'm not one for stopping at home. I don't like going out socially much, and I won't even go into town unless I'm forced to, but I like to go out to work. I've worked all the time I've been married. I've never been off as long as I've been off this time, even when the kiddies were little. I think that's why I looked forward to being off at first, but it wears off. But to be honest, I think I've stopped looking. It's just gradual, you get out of the habit, you don't bother. My husband used to tease me. He'd say, 'Go on, you don't really want to go back to work.' We've managed alright. I don't worry about it, but I mean we *just* manage, there's nothing left.

I don't go out a lot. I don't even go out a right lot for shopping actually. Because part of my husband's job is buying in for where he works at college and with us living away from town, he'll say, 'Do you want anything from town?' and he just picks it up. I suppose it doesn't help any. Well you think it's helping, but as time goes on it doesn't really. I think I've really got to push myself and try to do something about it. I see a job in the paper and I think that'd be alright, but I don't do anything about it. Yet I like to go out to work. It's just because I've been here that long my confidence has gone. I've got funny that way. I don't go visiting really, I've no one to visit. My friends have nearly all got jobs, the ones that I bothered with anyway and none of my family are close by, so I can't go and visit my sister. We've no transport now, the car's off the road. I don't really know when I last went out. I think it was around Christmas time. Then again there's not a lot of money to go out spending.

I would like a job. I can feel myself getting into this routine, and I'll have to snap out of it. I know that it's just picking up courage to snap out of it. But you don't just get jobs now, you have to go crawling for them. I hated it at the beginning. I was bored to tears. Every day I used to get fed up, but you get used to that boredom gradually, it's a way of life. I don't know whether I could face a lot of people now. I worried over you coming. I used to feel lonely, but there again I'm used to it. The radio is never off and I talk to my animals. I always have done. I wouldn't say I feel lonely now, six months ago yes, I got that fed up. I don't think about it when I'm on my own but when my husband is in at night, he soon falls asleep if he's sat, and sometimes I say, 'I'm fed up, I'm on my own all day and then you're asleep at night.' When I'm on my own I don't notice it so much I only notice it when someone is there, and I can't talk to them, it's more annoying. It's better to be on your own doing your jobs and letting your mind wander.

Mary Leason:

I was a supervisor at Roger Firth, I had been doing that for about nine months, and before that I had been a machinist. I was also shop steward for about ten years, but I had to give that up when I took the job as supervisor, I'd been with the company since I got married, before my son was born, and that's going back about 27 years. I left when I had him and then I went back. There were quite a few of us in fact that had worked for the old Roger Firth. When I'd left school, I worked at the Canadian Treasury in Lancaster and it closed down. Well, there wasn't a lot of work then so I went to work at the underwear factory and that's how I started in clothing. It was all there was at the time. Then I got married and came here and I went into the same trade at Roger Firth. When I left to have my son, I started working in the College, cleaning in the morning to get some extra money. When he was five, I started back at Roger Firth. To begin with, I didn't go in until nine o'clock but it was full time.

They'd offered me the supervisor's job before, but I wouldn't take it because it meant loss of pay for me. I was getting £80 a week in the supervisor's job but when I was on the machine I was getting about £96, so it was a big drop, but that's because I was fast and I could earn that amount. To someone else it would have been a promotion and a pay rise, but to me it wasn't. The main reason that I took the job in the end was because of the state we were in. Carrington Viyella started introducing 'minutes' which was alien to Roger Firth even though they did have a piece system. That was to be expected really because nearly all the factories are on minutes now and with me having been shop steward I knew a lot about it.

I got about £3,000 in redundancy, but that included ten weeks wages in lieu of notice, so it was about £2,600 really. We did invest my £3,000 in Granny Bonds. You could say we invested it, but really it's gone this year in loss of earnings. Up to starting this job five weeks ago, I've earned this year, £480, when I should have earned £4,000. Look at it that way. I registered as unemployed as soon as we finished, the week before Christmas, but I wasn't entitled to any benefit. I knew I wasn't, because I'd been paying a married woman's stamp. I thought there was no point in paying the full stamp really. A few years ago it changed and I could have gone on to the full stamp then, but at my age, with ten years to go before retirement, it wasn't worth paying. So we were left living on his dole – you see my husband lost his job before me.

It's a terrible thing being made redundant and after all those years. I don't think it was the money, actually he got more redundancy for eight years service than I got for 20. Really I think what hurt me most was that I've always worked, all my life. I've always put a lot into my work and I think I had this feeling of being finished. It's a terrible feeling and you can't know it unless you've experienced it. I got fanatical over the housework, I got silly over it really. I was just trying to fill my days and it got ridiculous – I'd go looking for bits on the carpet! I used to go out with the dog. I used to go up to the shops every morning. But I felt as if there was a shadow hanging over me. I didn't enjoy going out socially anymore, it spoilt my social life. I just felt as if I'd lost someone.

At first I hadn't been too worried. I'd marvellous references. But then I started looking for a job. I went for a job at Woolworth's, it was only a 16-hour job and I thought I'd get it, but I didn't. Then I'd written to the hospital because there was a friend of mine that works there and there was a vacancy coming up in the linen room for a machinist. Well I thought I'd all the qualifications and the man who was in charge took me down for an interview before the job had been advertised. Everything seemed alright and I was just waiting to have it confirmed, but when it came to it they decided to give it to a young girl. In fact she was one of my girls from Roger Firth. Seemingly, the Health Authority had sent out a circular to take young people on. It's my age you see . . . I was dreading another birthday. If you can put down 49 that's not too bad but once you get to 50, you might as well be 58, it strikes people the same.

Well I tried everywhere. I wrote everywhere. Believe me, there can't be an employer in Harrogate that hasn't got a letter from me somewhere in his drawer. I was out of work for four months and that was the worst time. How many times did I go to that Job Centre? One morning they rang me up and said to be there next day, no later than nine o'clock because they'd got me an interview at some place. When I got there the interview turned out to be for 11.30 so I had to sit in a coffee bar for two hours, it wasn't worth going home with the bus fares 25p each way. I told them that I'd never do that again and that they could arrange the interview first and then I'd come. They said they couldn't do that and so I said well I wouldn't come again, but I did.

Anyway, I finally got this job at Key Electronics. It was just a morning job, eight o'clock until 12.30. Believe me when I walked in there that morning I nearly died. They were lovely people but dirty. I mean we weren't clean at Roger Firth, but it was chemicals you see and the smell! I didn't think I'd stick it but I did. I sort of brainwashed myself into it, more because it was somewhere to go for a morning. Anyway, I'd started there in April and after four months, half of that place went and I went with it. I was made redundant again. I was out of work for about six to seven weeks. Then I got this job in catering at the hospital. I saw it in the paper. There were 40 or so after that one little job. We make up and serve up the meals. It's right alien to me and hard work, but I quite enjoy it. I like serving the patients. The pay is not good. The other girls make up their pay by working weekends, but I only work Mondays to Fridays. Well I say I don't do weekends, but I am working this Saturday and he's also asked me to work next Friday night, so that means I'll get home at two o'clock in the afternoon and then I'll have to go out again when I'm worn out, but I don't like to say no.

I do this job and I'm pretty quick but I'm a novice compared to the others. Sometimes I feel like a kid. Well it's a job I'd never have considered at one time, but now I'm glad of it. So you try, and you

79

daren't say no to anything. Really I should say employers should have it made now, because anyone who's been made redundant, they are only too eager to please.

I'm a lot down on money now. I'm working 32 ½ hours a week for £39 which isn't a lot is it, and that's paying the cheap stamp. It would be even less if I was paying the full stamp. It's supposed to be part time but it's not is it? It's only 30 hours in our contract but he's asked us to come in half an hour earlier every day. He's putting in these extra hours to get the work done but he hasn't put it into our contracts. Well what he did say, quite honestly, he was quite fair, because I was on about how seven o'clock wouldn't do me, and he said well if I could get in for 7.15 I'll pay you from seven o'clock, because with you not being full time I can't pay you overtime. So I get in for about 12 minutes past. So it's really a question of whether you're better off changing the contract or keeping it this way. If it changed I'd really have to be in for seven o'clock.

I start, as I say, just a bit after seven. We start straight away on the breakfasts. Making them up, loading them on to the trolleys and then we go up on to the wards to serve them. We get it all in again, get everything back down to the kitchen again and wash up – we've got a big dishwasher – and clear up. At ten o'clock we have a coffee break for ten minutes, but we try to make it half an hour, otherwise we're working six-and-a-half hours with only a ten-minute break. Mind you we really have to move to get that break. Sometimes we don't get it at all, it depends how many of us are on that day and who's on. But usually we do, if we go really fast and I mean fast. The sweat's pouring off us and we've no clothes on under our overalls. It's so hot in there, I can't imagine what it will be like in the summer.

After our break there's the kitchen to be scrubbed down, cookers, surfaces and walls. They get really filthy and greasy. We have to do that before we start on the dinners. We try to get the dinners up as fast as possible, because the sooner you get them out, the sooner you can finish. We get them laid up by 11.30, and we're up on the wards by twelve o'clock. We can't really give them out before then because no one's hungry. I think five minutes to twelve is the earliest we've ever managed. But sometimes you have to go and find the patients before it gets cold! We serve them up, clear them up as soon as we can and get the trolleys back down to the kitchen. We're not supposed to move the trolleys really, it's been classified as too heavy for women, but we usually do it. You can never find a porter when you want one but there's always someone off with back trouble. Then we wash up and clear up the kitchens again. We finish at 1.30, except that we never do, it's more like 1.45, but we only get paid until 1.30 and that's why we go so fast to get finished, I'm not kidding the pace is really fast. I used to think sewing was fast. There's no way I'll keep this up. I'm pretty tired when I get home.

Sometimes I think I'm an idiot. When I wasn't working I got into a routine and I just can't break that routine. So I come in one day and I'll do the bedroom and one day I'll do the lounge, one day the kitchen and so on. No matter how tired I am, I'll do it and fit in the cooking and washing as well. So I have my routine when I come in, get a quick lunch and I work until 4.50 so really I could be working full time, but the difference is that by 5.15, I've finished for the night and I've got my weekends when I'm more or less free. When I was working at Roger Firth I'd come in, tidy up, and by the time I'd done the meal and washed up, it would be eight o'clock and I'd be tired out. He'd [husband] help a bit, but he doesn't have a lot of time. Really I had to do all the housework at weekends. Now I have a nice routine. I've got used to having my afternoons and weekends free, but I suppose, if I worked full time now, I'd still come home and do my routine.

I never wanted part-time work, it just happened like that I suppose. But I'm grateful to have this job, very grateful. I know I couldn't manage off his wage, some people have to and I sympathise. We've got to be more careful. I did mind losing my independence. I felt that I was taking what he earned, although we've always shared everything, I just felt that I wasn't pulling my weight.

I've had to change my lifestyle. I mean I get up now at six o'clock every morning. Well he has to as well, because he takes me to work. We've always been used to a holiday at Christmas but now I've got to work Christmas Day and New Year, they both fall on a Friday, and I work Fridays. I miss the people from Roger Firth, we worked together so long that we'll never get that sort of relationship again. You may go to another job, but you can't feel your natural self somehow, perhaps I will in time.

I do like this job. I didn't think that I would. They're very nice people but I come home exhausted. I liked the supervisor's job and I would like another job like that. I don't really feel like going back on to a machine now, although I always said that I could stay on a machine until I was 75. I mean they did used to stay on the machines until that age, but I don't think I'll be able to do this when I'm that old. I think I've got used to having less money and I find that I have more time to myself. So I do like that, but I mean things could change again. He wasn't out of work long and he's working for the council now, but you know what a state they're in. They've been asking for early retirements and now they're after voluntary redundancies. So you just don't know anymore.

Anne McKenzie:

I was a passer at Roger Firth, that's quality control. All the finished garments came to me and I'd put them on a dummy and I had to inspect them to see if there were any faults. I used to get about £45 to £50 for that, take home pay that is. I used to think it wasn't fair because the passers got a percentage of the machinists' output, so if they had a bad day, we had a bad day. But I liked it there. I was there over five years. Funnily enough, my mother worked there when I was a kid. When I first left school I went to work in a building contractors firm as an office junior. I worked my way up and ended up on the switchboard which I liked. I started when I was 16 and left at 18 because I was pregnant. I got married and left work as well. Well I worked right up to having Lucy, then I didn't work again until she was about two. Then I put her in this day nursery and I got a job in the Milk Marketing Board in the laboratory. It was nice there and it was just along the road. I was there for three years until Lucy was five and went to school.

She went from nursery school to school and then I had to do part-time work. I've worked in an hotel as a domestic, I've helped in schools at dinner times with the school meals. I worked for a while with a small clothing firm round here. Then I went down to London and lived there for about three-and-a-half years and Lucy went to school there. I worked for a blouse manufacturer. I enjoyed doing that. Then I came back here and I got the job with Firth's through the employment office. So I've always worked really, there were just those couple of years when I didn't.

There had been a lot of talk about closing down, but I don't think I was thinking that far ahead. Really we did quite well with redundancy pay and I thought it would keep me going for a while. I thought surely I'll be able to find a job. I've never had any problems before. Then all of a sudden I was out of work. It happened all so quickly and actually when I sat there and thought I wouldn't be going back any more, that's when it hit me. I wasn't too worried because I knew I had this money to rely on. I got £1,000 all told, which wasn't bad, and I thought if I didn't get a job in three months then I could sign on and I was entitled to benefit. But really I thought I'd get a job and I didn't. I went after so many jobs and had so many interviews. In shops, all kinds of shops and then there was a job for a care assistant in an old people's home. I applied for that along with another thousand applicants. I applied for three jobs in old people's homes, in fact. I couldn't believe it when I went for these interviews, the number of people after them and it was always the same thing, 'Well, we have so many more people to interview, we'll have to let you know, and if you don't hear from us by such and such a time, then you can take it that you were not successful.' This used to go on and on. You'd set off for these interviews full of confidence and when you came out – it was terrible.

Then of course I had domestic problems. You see we were divorced in 1974, and that's when I went to live in London. When I came back we lived together for another five, nearly six years. I think they were the happiest times, we were more happy then, than when we were actually married. I was working full time and I had £40 going into the bank every week which I could save, or spend on myself and Lucy, or on the home, because we could live on his money. We used to go on holiday while I was working at Firth. We got some good holidays, which we wouldn't have been able to afford if I hadn't been working. We used to go out a lot socially, we had a nice car and we were able to buy clothes. Then all of a sudden everything just seemed to crumble, it all folded up, he left, he recently got married again, I lost my job. I felt shattered because I had nothing left . . . I was here on my own. I was sitting in the house all day, all night and I was really down and I used to think, if only I could get a job, and I did try . . . the two things seemed to happen together.

Financially it was very hard. You see when he left me I was still at Roger Firth and on short time. I was working three days, two days and sometimes only one, so my wages were really down and that was the only money I had. Lucy hadn't left school then and the only other bit of income was the family allowance. I think we were existing on under £40 a week and that was with the family allowance. Of course I had the rent rebate which was a big help, and the rest I used to try and allow for. I used to think, 'God, the gas and electric bills', they'd always come at the same time. Then of course there was the telephone. I didn't want to give up the telephone because I do feel as if I've got contact with people, because I don't go out at all. In fact people would find it hard to believe I never went out. Then there was the rental on the television but, thank God, I didn't owe anything to hire purchase. I do smoke. I used to buy cigarettes and that was the only thing. It was a bit better when Lucy left school and we were both unemployed. I had earnings related that was added on which made it a little bit more – it worked out as £52 a fortnight. And then when Lucy left school she was able to claim straight away and her money was £30 a fortnight. So that's what we were living on. She got her money the opposite week to me, so that by the time it came round to getting her money I was there with my hand out sort of thing because mine . . . had all gone. I'd put my redundancy pay in the building society at first, and I was trying to live off the other money that I got, severance pay and that – about one hundred and odd pounds. I thought that would see me through over Christmas, but from

February some time I started dipping into the building society.

It was nice during the winter, not having to go out in the bad weather. I didn't have to get up early in the cold mornings, that was the *only* thing I can honestly say that I enjoyed. It's a long time from December to August. I decorated, I spent quite a lot of time decorating. I used to find things to do in the morning, it was the afternoon that dragged. But I used to go out walking with Ben (the dog). I used to go miles. My mother lives round the corner, and I'd go round there. I decorated her flat whilst I was off. Towards the end, they were just long days, especially if you didn't see anybody. I did the garden, nobody else would do it, so I had to. I relaxed and sat in the garden when it was a nice sunny day. I read the paper, read a book. Oh I must have read hundreds of books. I think I only went into town once a fortnight, when I had to sign on. It was the only time I went into town because I didn't have any money.

Then, you won't believe this, having been all that time without a job, I got two jobs. So I had to sit down and think about it, which was the best one. One was at the hospital, as an auxillary in the psycho-geriatric ward and that meant shift work and travelling. The other was in a supermarket and that would be just a walk around the corner. Anyway, I wanted the hospital job, I took that one and now I'm glad I did. The shifts don't worry me you see, because I've no ties. I do two shifts: 7.45 to 4.15 and 12.15 to nine o'clock. In a week you do alternate shifts. You only work $37\frac{1}{2}$ hours a week. You're still getting your time off even if you have to work Saturdays and Sundays, you get two days off in the week and every so often you get a long weekend. I get tired because it's hard work, they're not patients that are in bed. They're not always old people, some of them are young. They're lovely people and I do like the job.

You need a sense of humour for this job. There was one patient who was going through this aggressive stage and I had her on the toilet. She must wear trousers this particular lady, she gets agitated if she's showing her knees. So I had her on the toilet and I was down pulling her trousers off and she said she'd seen mice running around behind me, and she shouted, 'Oh don't let it come near me, I'll kill it,' and she hit me over the head with her slipper. It knocked me off my balance and my cap was all bashed in. She was all pent up you could see and she went like that . . . and clawed my face. Well I came out of that toilet with my hat bashed in and my face dripping with blood! But you can't bear them any malice, they're like children. You get others that are more sensible and they're like mothers to the rest of them. You get them going off hand in hand together and they'll say, 'We'll be going home now, we'll just get our coats, we'll see you again sometime,' and they trot off down the ward hand in hand. They can't get out, it's locked you see. Sometimes I come home really shattered. By the time you're ready to come off you think, 'God, let me out of here!' Sometimes if you've had a bad day you think, 'God, for what I'm earning.' Some days to be crude, you can be up to your armpits in shit! You do get all the dirty jobs. Every day you earn your money.

We don't earn a lot. Now when I first started the job they told me it would be six weeks before I got paid and I thought, I can't go on all that time. Anyway they said I could ask for a loan and they said £100 loan would be no problem, they ended up giving me £60. Well it was ridiculous and I was borrowing off my mother and I mean she's only on a pension herself. When I finally did get my pay, I couldn't believe it. I had £199 for six weeks work. They had taken £178 stoppages off me. There was the £60 loan, but I'd paid £71 income tax, £17 national insurance, £22 superannuation, plus the transport and union fee. So that left me with £199. Now the council wants a statement of earnings so they can assess whether I'm still entitled to any rent rebate! I'm sort of getting used to the money now. The hourly rate is £1.69 and I get a basic pay of £275 and then additions, weekend duties and evening duties and that, brings it up to £322 a month, but then by the time everything is taken off I end up with £221 to put into the bank. But all the girls are the same, we all grumble about pay. But we won't be coming out on strike, not in our ward. We all agreed not to because in a psychiatric ward you just can't leave them. I mean it's like walking out on a room full of children.

I manage fairly well because with being paid monthly one advantage I find is that I've got that lump sum to pay off bills. I'm always overdue but at least I can pay them. I have to make my money last the month, so I have to sort of work it out and plan. I've never got any spare. But I'm not worrying about money like I did before. As long as I can keep working, as long as I've an income, I know somehow, I will pay my bills. If I have to leave one to pay another, I'll do it that way. The telephone got paid, even though I got the disconnection card. Now I've got the gas and electric again. I will have to pay them out of next month's money, that'll be £70, then there's the television rental, so really the first £100 is always spoken for in bills and the rest of whatever I get will be for living. I've let the television slide for two months and I owe my mother £60.

I always used to go to the hairdressers, because I did like to have my hair done. I used to have it streaked out but I can't afford that now. The only reason I go to the hairdressers now is to have it cut. I don't buy clothes for myself, I don't actually go out to the shops anymore. I think it must be a year since I actually bought myself anything from the shops. I got one of these catalogues this year and that's the way I have to do it. I'm hoping that I should be able to afford a night out and a hairdo.

I still don't go out a lot socially, for the first few months I was sorting myself out, but I don't go out now because I'm not bothered at the moment. I could go out with the girls I work with, there's quite a social life up there, but I don't really bother much. By the time I get home from work, if I'm on lates, it's 9.30 and I'm tired. I've had a long day and I'm glad to be home. At the moment I'm happy as I am and it suits me working these kinds of hours, what else would I be doing. Now I'm working, I'm enjoying my freedom. I've started to enjoy my home again, enjoying the fact that I don't have to answer to anybody. The money that's in the bank is my money and I do what I wish with it. I'm quite happy. It's a lot easier now that it's just me and Lucy. I don't have to rush in and start cooking meals, and she's good. She does quite a lot of housework and she'll do the washing. She leads her own life, she has a boyfriend and he's a nice boy, but I'd hate it if she married young like me, that would really upset me.

I'd hate to be out of work again. Sometimes I may go into town with Lucy because she has to sign on and when we go into the labour exchange, I feel it . . . it brings it all back to me. I mean one day I might not want to go on working, I don't know, I might get sick of the whole thing. But I think I'll always work. I've always been so independent even when I was married. It was a case of having to be really. A job like this would be difficult if you're married, if your husband's at home weekends and you're at work. I don't want to stay like this forever though. I'd like to think that somewhere I could start a relationship with somebody because I don't want to be on my own all my life. In terms of meeting someone and having a relationship, or getting married again, I just can't see it. Sometimes when I'm coming home from work, I think well that's another day over. Sometimes I feel a bit let down coming home and there's only me and the dog, I think he's my best friend at the moment. That's sometimes how I feel, but I don't really let it get me down. I feel as if I'm missing out on something sometimes, but then again I don't. I value my independence. I'd like a man to take me out and for company, but I don't want to be washing his socks.

Rachel Lloyd:

When I left school I worked in a florists for a year. I'd already been working there on Saturdays. Then I went to Roger Firth. My friend had said they needed someone. When I was on stitching I was earning about £80 a week, but just before I left I went on to vents, and then I was getting about £55 a week. I didn't mind it when I was doing edge stitching, there was no problem, but vents! They said it was because I was left-handed but I don't think it was, I just never clicked with the job at all. I used to get big rails of coats back that I'd done wrong. I think I'd been on edge stitching so long, I was used to rushing them through. I was trying to rush vents and I was cutting them up to the armhole. It used to make me sick because I was getting told off every day. I couldn't get it right. I would have left in January anyway. I was pregnant. So it worked out right for me. I think I was the only one it benefited really. It was funny really with me being pregnant, because all the time the rumours were going round I was thinking, I hope we do, because it meant me leaving with a lot of money. Really I felt sorry for all the girls because they wouldn't be able to get another job. I got nearly £1,000 in redundancy pay and everything. When we did get redundant I was really bored from that time to having Tracy. It was three months and it was horrible.

I didn't register as unemployed when I first left work, but I did when I had her. My husband – he's a plasterer – was unemployed at the time you see, so he could have looked after her. He was unemployed for ten months and I was getting worried about money then. It was hard. He was getting £22 a week and when I signed on I got the same. I went after two or three jobs but then he got a job when she was three months old. It was horrible before he got that job. We got behind with rent and everything. With being pregnant and all, I wanted all this baby stuff, and on what he was getting [Unemployment Benefit] you couldn't do it. A lot of my redundancy went on big stuff, like the cot and pram and we had a little bit left over and we bought things that we knew we'd never be able to afford again. We both had clubs at the time, so we finished them off so we wouldn't have any debts at all and we'd got a wardrobe on HP so we paid that off. We finished paying his motorbike off that he had then. I still owe my mum £50 from then. I always had people helping, my mum used to come down and give me stuff, food and that.

We used to have a lot of arguments. All we ever argue about really is money. I think if we hadn't have had her then it would have been worse – well it might not have been because I'd have been able to get a job. He liked to go out a lot, well he still does. Not night-clubbing every night, but he goes out quite a lot, and he couldn't afford to do anything really. For about two months I don't think we had a proper meal. We used to have beans on toast or egg and bacon, or something. It was ages before we had stewing meat or anything like that. We used to plod on really, we just got used to never having anything. Even now I have to watch my money. It takes some getting used to. Now I think, 'I'd better not buy that.' I've sort of got used to not having my own wage. I don't miss it as much as I did. Anything I want now I have to ask him for it. It used to get me depressed at first, knowing I hadn't got £5 to buy anything. I never go out anyway so I don't need anything new really. I think I might have done part time if Roger Firth were still going. Sometimes I think I wouldn't mind getting a part-time job, because Pete's mum said she would always look after her for me. But then with having Tracy I wouldn't just go out and do anything for money, it would have to be something I really wanted to do. I 'phoned up about one, a sewing job, but I thought it would be as boring as the one I was doing at Roger Firth really. I wouldn't want to just leave her, especially now, you'd miss everything that they're doing. There's no point anyway now, I've just found out that I'm pregnant again.

Now we've got Tracy there's a lot more housework to do. Most things I don't mind, but ironing I hate. You have more time as a matter of fact, but it goes that quick you don't notice it. I find it easier now even though I've got a baby. I can take my own time doing it, whereas when I was working, I'd get home at 5.15 or something, and straight away do the tea, then wash up and then I'd have to start everything at night, washing and so on. Now I can start when I want. There's a lot more work now, but it seems to equal out. You've got all day to do it, when you've got the time. When we were both unemployed he didn't do anything then, I was seven months pregnant and still had to do everything. After about two or three weeks I used to say, 'You're off work, you should be doing it.' When I stopped nagging he started to do it. Then we shared most of the time, although I think half the time it was boredom. Women can occupy themselves more than men I think. Women will do anything. They'll go and rake a cupboard out or look around shops, but fellas don't. They just tend to sit there and stew in it when they're out of work.

He was a great help to me when I first had Tracy. He used to take her out and get up in the night to her when I started to bottle feed her, and get up first thing in the morning with her to feed her. She's so good for him. They always say girls go for their dads, but sometimes it gets me really mad. I don't feel so pushed out now because she does play him up sometimes but I felt if I went back to work and left them two together, I might as well not bother coming back home, just leave them to it. He gets her up in the morning whether she's awake or not. He'll change a nappy, but not a messy one. I thought it was a novelty at first and I thought it would wear off but it hasn't. He's really good for a fella. He's right short tempered most of the time and he quite surprised me really when we had her how different he was. I thought he'd be one of those that would moan about the noise all the time. It was a bit hard when he got a job because I didn't know what it was like looking after her all day. When he's unemployed he does everything, meals and what have you, but whenever he's in work, he does nothing.

Well he's out of work again actually – not long really, about a month. He got made redundant again. I'm not quite sure yet what we're getting [in benefit], we should be getting some supplement and that. It's not so bad because with him being in work for that while, we got paid up with bills, but when the next big electric bill comes, we'll have to rake round to pay that. But it's been alright this time really. Before we were only getting about £30 a week for us all and she was so little then and she was still having such a lot bought, her own sort of food and that, but now she has some of what we have. I think because Pete didn't have a job for a right long time, it was a matter of making the most of it while it was there, sort of thing. Get things paid up because we know he's going to be out of work again . . . it's happened that many times. My mum still helps out. Like at Easter, Tracy only got one Easter egg, and everybody bought her little socks and dresses and things like that.

I miss the company from Roger Firth, because working in a factory full of lasses, I think it was just a good laugh all the time really. We were working but we never sat and seriously worked half the time. When I first left work I missed it more. There were a few of them that went to the hospital and I used to think how they'd all be down there, like we were at Roger Firth, in fag room, smoking and laughing and messing about, but I don't know really. I could never go back to that now, not that sort of job at Roger Firth. The same thing over and over again each day. I think that's why you have such a good laugh in a place like that, because if you didn't you'd just go loopy with frustration. I miss the lasses I suppose . . . I miss lasses night out, we used to have some good ones, you know, loads of lasses on nights out. I don't know, my friends are different now to what they were then, everything's changed so much. Now it's all baby talk all the time, kids and that and how different they are and what one's doing. The two really good friends that I had, they're still in full-time work and they work together so in a way I felt a bit pushed out from them because I was leaving to have a baby and they think babies are boring. I've changed so much in what I do and their lives haven't changed at all. All I've got to talk about to them is her, because that's all I ever do you see. It's like when she started walking, I told all my friends – 'She's walking now,' 'Oh yes' they said . . . and yet to you it's the biggest thing in the world.

There's no way really I'm going to work again, not until she's at school anyway. Not with two. Well I don't think I will. When I was signing on I thought I might get a job, I won't be a housewife – I didn't really think of myself as a housewife anyway – but that was before she was walking. There's more to do now. We go to the swings and run about the field. I enjoy looking after her more now. I don't want to miss anything really. When she's at school and maybe this next one's at playschool, I'll maybe get a morning job or something. I think I'd need to then to fill the gap. I wouldn't know what to do all day, there'd be nothing to do except normal housework. I think before we needed the money so much, and that was the main reason I wanted a job. I mean we could still do with the money, but I think it's not worth giving up – I mean sometimes she drives me nuts but most of the time it doesn't bother me. It's funny really because I know this woman and her little girl is only a month older and she's always saying to me, 'Don't you miss being able to go out and not having to bother about babysitters,' as if she really hates it, being a mother. I just say, 'No.' I mean as soon as she was born, I just accepted it as part of my life now. Sometimes when I'm talking to her it makes me feel guilty for enjoying looking after her.

I get these parents' magazines and I read in there about these women whose houses become prisons, you know, and I can't really understand what it's like. But I can imagine it really getting on top of you if you don't see anybody else, you're on your own with them all day. It's no wonder you get these child batterers and that. Because I mean she's really good most of the time, for her age and that, she's quite good to look after, just a bit stubborn, but they all are, but I've seen some kids that would drive me nuts. I don't love it all the time, there are times when I could easily dump her off at my mum's for the weekend when she's getting on my nerves. I think most of that is because I'm pregnant and I've got so much on my mind, so much to do.

I get out quite a lot. I think if I didn't know anybody to go and see, I'd hate it. There's my mum, and Pete's mum and my grandmother and they're my family that I go and see. I see them about once a week each. Then I've got a couple of close friends that I know really well, that I used to know years ago, school time. I don't like stopping in. I get everything done in the morning, and then go out especially when it's nice weather. The days go quickly really.

I feel I never want to work again, well not at the moment. To me it seems sort of humdrum again – working. When I first had Tracy I used to love just going out in my own time to see people and things like that. I always say if I ever went back to work I'd never go back on piece-work, where you have to get so many out by dinner time and all this. That's one thing I enjoy about not working, doing it in my own time, at my own pace. I could never go back to that sort of job at Roger Firth. I think really I wouldn't like to go back to the routine of work. You still sort of get into a routine even if you're at home all the time, ironing builds up, beds all need changing and stuff like that, but I wouldn't really like to go back to work, you know, get the same bus every day, come in every day at the same time. I think I get more fulfilment out of looking after her than doing a job where I'm doing the same thing every day. If I did go back to work it would have to be something really interesting, really different.

5
A Working Life

What started off as a study of redundancy and unemployment becomes a study of employment as well, because it is impossible to understand the impact of job loss on women without understanding both the conditions under which women work and what paid work means to women. This is equally true for men, but the difference is that for men the connection between employment and unemployment is *assumed*, whereas for women it is not. Unemployment for men is acknowledged to be a problem of considerable proportions. The loss of a man's wage can often mean the loss of a family's major source of income and male unemployment is therefore a major cause of family poverty. Moreover, the problems are not only economic. Psychologically, unemployment can hit at the very roots of men's self esteem and masculine identity. This happens because, for men, work is *central* in making sense of men's lives. It is a component of masculinity (Cockburn, 1983; Tolson, 1977). Unemployment is not just the loss of a wage, it is the loss of a 'breadwinner's' wage and a place amongst men. Work and masculinity are so entangled that in unemployment men are not only workless, they are seemingly unsexed. They have lost the very point of their existence as men, to work to support a family.

Conversely, there is a common assumption that women do not suffer in unemployment, both because the loss of their wage will not have such ramifications for the family, and because their femininity is not so tied into work. Women now make up a large proportion of the workforce and are in employment for most of their adult lives, with only a relatively short break for childbirth and childcare. Yet the increased participation of women in the labour force has occurred without apparently eroding the ideology of domesticity and maternalism, which squarely constructs a woman's role and femininity within the home and family. Women go out to work, but they remain tethered to the family, ideologically and in practice through their unpaid domestic labour. It is still women's work and it has neither diminished nor been shared with men. It has been argued that this ongoing location of women in the family to perform domestic labour, has resulted in them being a more exploitable source of labour and has allowed for the marginalisation of women's employment (Barrett, 1980; Beechey, 1978). It certainly allows for the assumption that women do not suffer in unemployment as men do. Simply, it is held that in unemployment women are economically supported by their men and occupied by domestic activities. If anything, unemployment might resolve the implicit tension of their double life. As in employment so it is in unemployment that familial ideology comes to the forefront in interpreting women's job loss. Here it is the *nexus* of family and work which so crucially influences women's experiences of unemployment.

Married Women Working

The single most dramatic change that has taken place in the pattern of women's employment in the post-war period is that childbirth and raising a family is not the end of a woman's working life. Increasingly, women have returned to work once their children reach school age. The majority of women with children from Harrogate and Castleford conformed to this pattern. The crucial ingredient is to find work that fits into school hours:

> When I had our family I finished work and I stayed at home for nine years. I didn't believe in leaving them and going out to work. I stayed with them because I always got pleasure out of them. It was a bit of a struggle. Then when my eldest was nine I went back to work, part time. I worked 9.30 to three o'clock. I used to take them to school, pick them and bring them home.

I left work when I had my first child. Then with nobody about [to help] I didn't work at all. I'd nobody to fall back on, like grannies. So I took my first job when they were at school. My youngest was seven. It was great because I worked from ten o'clock to three o'clock and all the holidays I used to have off. I think it's essential for your children to know that you're there.

I started when the children started school. They were good, they let me come in when I could and then as the children got older, I gradually worked up my hours.

I went back to work when she started school at four-and-a-half. I worked in Woolworth's for two years. The manager let me go in at 9.05, because I had to take Suzanne to school and then a new manager came and we had to be behind the counter by nine. Well, that made all the difference to me. I left and went to Roger Firth. I went part time. They were good like that, but it was worth their while really. Sometimes they got more out of someone who worked 30 hours, than someone who worked 40 hours.

It is unusual for women to return to full-time manual work after having a baby, simply because it is practically too difficult. If, however, decent childcare arrangements can be made, it is often easier to combine full-time work with very small children. School hours dictate women's hours, whereas the provision of care for preschool children can be more flexible. 'When I had my daughter I was home six months. We'd just got used to living on one wage and then he was out of work. A friend of mine looked after Anna, so I could work. My husband was not too happy about it, but he more or less accepted it after a few weeks. I was full time at first and when she started school at five I went part time.' The restatement of the ideology of motherhood after the Second World War propped up the State's failure to meet women's need for preschool childcare provision. When a woman says: 'I don't believe in women leaving young children. I do think a woman needs to be at home, until a child starts school at least. I think they miss a lot, they miss their babyhood', she is not simply 'buying' the ideology. However, it can indeed be very rewarding and pleasurable to have and look after small children; especially in contrast to much of the soul destroying, boring and monotonous work that so many women are forced into. It can be one of the most positive and rewarding periods of a woman's life. The problems arise with the privatisation of childcare, isolation and the lack of choices. In the absence of socialised childcare provision, if women want to return to work before their children are at school they have to both find private solutions and face ostracism. At school age that changes. The State takes responsibility for the *education* of children from the age of five, and then, as an unintended consequence, both makes it alright for women to leave their children, and provides State-socialised childcare. This provision has allowed millions of women in Britain to enter paid employment by the back door.

Once the period of the intensive care of children is over, the next stage is to provide a decent standard of living for them and that is purchased through the women's wage. In the 1950s and 1960s women, working-class women especially, began to return to work to acquire for their children the education, experiences and opportunities that they themselves had never had (Jephcott *et al.*, 1962; Zweig, 1952). Married women return to work not for themselves but for their children, and femininity is saved. Work is not a negation of women's role, rather the 'new femininity' *includes* paid work as one aspect of being a wife and mother.

When I first started going out to work, I had the four children at home. And with four children growing up they were quite expensive. For instance, my eldest daughter wanted to do typing and shorthand, and my money paid for her to have lessons.

I mainly went back to work so that we could afford a holiday, but then Steven was at school until he was 18 and so was my daughter and it was very hard. I don't know what I'd have done if I hadn't been working at that time. They couldn't have had what they did really.

I've always worked because I've had to. I don't know where the idea that women work for pin money comes from. When my sons were young they both had a good education, both of them had special tutoring which I couldn't have done if I hadn't worked. I couldn't have given them the education if I hadn't worked, it would have been impossible on one wage. People work because they have to work, I don't think anybody does it for any other reason. I think it's always been essential for anyone who wanted the better things in life, for a woman to work as well.

For some women the sheer necessity of working to support their children is even more apparent:

I've had to do these things. You see I've got seven children. I got married at 16 and I'd had five of them by the time I was 21. He was a seaman my husband – my first husband – and he came from Skye. Well the women walk three paces behind their husbands up there. Then he started drinking heavily and when he was at home it was nothing to him to drink a bottle of whisky in the morning and then start ructions in the house. He set fire to the house once with the kids in it. The trouble really started when the kids started to grow up. The girls were about 14 and wanted to go to dances, buy clothes and wear make-up and all that, and men get awfully jealous of their girls. He wouldn't let them go out and chased the boys away. So anyway I didn't see why my kids should have to put up with that, so I left. I had seven kids when I left him and they were all going to school. Since then I've always worked to support them. I've never claimed any money off him because I didn't want him to know where I was.

It is childbearing which biologically divides men and women, but the socially-constructed sexual division of labour between men and women hinges on childcare and housework. Until the responsibility for childcare and housework shifts from being women's alone, it continues both to justify women's existence in the home and confines them there. Yet nothing stays the same for ever and even this seemingly intractable domestic division has changed in some respects. At one time it was housework alone which justified a woman's existence in the home. Women gave up work on marriage in order to care for and service their man. The children came along and were equal recipients of women's labour of love. Now housework alone is not a reason for staying at home, and women's role, which was once to service her wage earner, is now also to share with him the task of earning that wage. The increase in the number of married women at work bears witness to this change. What is easily forgotten now, is the sheer volume of domestic labour women still perform, *and* largely for the domestic convenience of men. Women's paid work is made possible by a finely tuned, highly 'taylorised' domestic 'routine'. Aided by pressure cookers, electric oven timers and late-night shopping, women perform and undertake an exhausting work load. It has been intensified and reorganised, but not reduced nor shared:

> I do as much as I can before I go to work in the morning, because I'm so tired when I come home. I go out at lunch time, we only have half an hour, and do the shopping. The big shopping I call for on my way home. I tend to prepare the meals the night before. Washing I do at the weekends. Big jobs, washing, windows, ironing, I do on Sundays. I'm not a religious person.

> When I get up in the morning, I've not much to do because I've done it the night before. I get his shirt and things out, and I do the breakfast things before I go to bed. When I come home from work on the night time, I do an evening meal. If I have some washing I do that then. If it is summer time I peg it out, if not, I put it out the following morning before I go to work. Friday night I go to the late-night opening to do the shopping, my big shop, and the rest will be done at the weekend. I've accepted that

I have to do it and that's it. I think if you sit and think, 'Oh, I've got to do so and so,' it makes you feel worse, whereas if you get on with it, it's soon done.

Women perform a bone-grinding schedule of work without any significant assistance from men:

If I was ill he'd do it, but because I'm at work and he doesn't want me to go out to work, I have to fit it in for myself. I wouldn't ask him. It would be an excuse for him to say if you can't do your housework, don't go out to work. I'd have to be ill, I'd have to be dying! He's washed up sometimes. If he wants to get to the sink and I've not washed up, then he will.

Sometimes on a Sunday afternoon he might wash up, but he's hopeless. It's harder work trying to get him to do it, than doing it yourself.

He doesn't do anything unless I ask him. He'll wash the pots and leave them draining. I'll say to him you can bring the washing in. If I didn't say it to him, it wouldn't dawn on him to do it. It's not that he's lazy, it's just that he doesn't think. I think it's more or less my fault. I did everything from when I first got married and I think if you do that you sort of burden yourself.

Where men do participate they tend to be rather selective in what they do: 'He likes cooking. He likes to cook a meal, but he wouldn't wash up, won't vacuum, nor make the beds. He's not domesticated.' Occasionally the oddity occurs, a man who does most of the housework, and there is a reason for this unusual behaviour: 'My husband does the cooking, he makes the dinner, plus he tidies up for me, vacuums round, makes the bed. He does the basic things every day. I'm lucky that way. I think why it came about was, unfortunately when he was 17, his mother was taken to hospital with TB and my husband was the only one you see, so he had to buckle in and look after himself and his dad. So he had a pretty good training.' On the whole however, not only do men not participate in domestic work they produce, but they also require special attention themselves:

> I've worked all my married life, except for those months when I had Anna. He's the sort of person who likes to feel he's being looked after. As long as he's got clean things to wear and he's got a meal to come home to, then I'm giving him attention and in that respect he's alright. But if I didn't bother with him and he thought I was just getting on with my job, then he'd feel neglected. He sometimes turns round and says, 'Don't get doing too much, you'll make yourself poorly!' I do get run down. I have to take extra iron and calcium sometimes.

Men require the kind of servicing which in the end forced one woman with grown-up children to change her full-time job for a part-time one:

> My husband would have got worse. You see when I was at Roger Firth I came in at 4.40, and he came in at five o'clock, so it worked out nicely. I was here to do his tea and his breakfast. With the new job I was working until eight o'clock of a night one week and starting at seven o'clock in the morning the other week. I tried always to have something in the oven for when he came in and things like that. I'm lucky really because he doesn't say, 'You can't do this or that', because he knows if I really want to do it, I'd do it. But he was getting a bit mad. It quietened him down when I said I'd get this part-time job.

There are probably both class and generational differences amongst men in the amount of housework they will undertake. Castleford, in particular, is not just a working-class town, but a coal-mining town, the very heartland of masculinity (See Dennis *et al.*, 1979). Amongst young married couples without children it was noticeable that men did a little more housework than their older counterparts, but once a woman stayed at home, having had a baby, there was a slide into a more orthodox allocation of the domestic routine. Once at home, women inevitably take on more and more of the domestic work.

> He'd vacuum and make the beds, wash out the bathroom. I'd just say, 'Well you do this and I'll do this.' Or if we got home at the same time, he'd make the tea, while I did my work. Now I can manage it all during the day. When I was working I was trying to fit it all in. Now I've got my days planned out for each job.

> Some evenings he'd cook the meal. Or while I'd clean up, he'd polish or hoover. We'd muck in together. We shared it. We've got a very good relationship I'm glad to say. He'll still wash up of an evening, or cook the meal if I'm busy with the baby.

The absence of a husband, or male wage earner, however, can make quite a difference to domestic life. Somehow the volume of work is less and children are enlisted, boys and girls, to help out. There is no model of masculinity in the house to stamp its mark on the allocation of tasks: 'I've always made my boys do their own bedrooms. And they'd do jobs for me as they got older. My boys can clean this house better than any girl. I've got a friend and her boys do nothing and the girls clean up and do the dishes. Those boys don't move a cup. Well I don't believe in that. My husband was brought up lazy.'

Young Women

While married women with children combine domestic labour with paid work, the working lives of young women are not unaffected by the 'promise' of femininity. Young working-class women have few options. Jobs are not chosen, they happen:

> They kept asking you what you'd like to do and I kept saying I'd like to work with children and they kept saying wouldn't you like to work in a factory, and I ended up in a factory.

102

At the time it was the only thing going.

I thought of being a model. I was a beauty queen you see, but my mum wouldn't let me. I'll stay in tailoring now, the money's good and me and my boyfriend are almost engaged. You can always get work in tailoring.

Their low wages keep them in the family, where they have little autonomy: 'She's right funny about me going out, with me being the only girl you see, she doesn't realise that I have to go out, I'm 18 you see. One minute she's saying, "Please yourself," the next minute she's trying to stop me going out. I never bring boys home.' Young women are marking time: 'I don't have a regular boyfriend, but I've started saving me bottom drawer and things like that.' They are both 'saved by, and locked within, the culture of femininity' (McRobbie, 1978). Their stifling existence within working-class family life and in unskilled work is escaped through an ideology of romance and marriage. Their release will be through a man and children of their own. It is in fact their only real option and romanticism convinces them that their marriage will not be anything like their mother's, and their family quite unlike the one from which they need to escape.

Young *married* women are marking time, in an even more specific way. It is a time when they are both seeking to maximise their income and are the least committed to working. They are nest building. They are preparing for the fulfilment of women's role.

Unemployment

The women from Roger Firth were variously married, single, divorced and widowed, of a range of ages, with and without dependent children. There cannot be a *single* experience of unemployment shared by all women. As for men, the impact varied according to personal circumstances. As women, the extent to which they could be supported and occupied by the family, depended both on whether women had a family to support them, and whether they were at a point in their life cycle where they could or would want to be reabsorbed by domesticity. Women's position in the family and with regard to the domestic routine, changes over the life cycle and cannot necessarily reconcile women to unemployment. On the contrary there are certain stages of a woman's life cycle, where work and wage earning is particularly significant and unemployment can only be a difficult experience.

Supported by the family?

The most common assumption that is made about female unemployment is that it does not cause the same financial hardship as it does for men. It is assumed therefore that it does not matter that many married women are not entitled to any kind of social security benefit whilst unemployed. Their husbands will of course support them.

When it can, the family *does* offer support to unemployed members, be they wives, husbands or children:

It probably wasn't quite so bad for myself, and others like me who were married, because we had our husbands at work. It was a case of adjusting really.

Well I got rid of the car, but I've not had real difficulties because my wife's the main wage earner now.

I didn't think I'd be able to manage so me mum said if I ever got stuck she'd help me out so that eased it a bit you know. Me mum and dad said not to worry and if I couldn't afford to pay me board or 'owt, they'd keep me until I found a job.

However, many women are not in households where they are supported in this way. In neither town were men the sole 'breadwinners' for their families and moreover, a male wage was, all too often, inadequate to provide the sole family support. More commonly, a woman's wage was a crucial component of family household income, whilst a substantial minority of women live in households *not* headed by a man. Whether divorced, separated, widowed or unmarried, many women are dependent on their own wage-earning capacity.

The impact of job loss amongst those men and women who lost their jobs with the closures of the Roger Firth factories varied in the very first instance through variations in material circumstances. It was women on their own who were the group most vulnerable to poverty through job loss. Totally dependent on their own wage, State welfare proved to be an inadequate alternative provision. They only 'managed' by having unheated houses, going nowhere, and eating little.

I was earning about £90 a week at Roger Firth and I found that quite adequate. When I signed on I started with £27 a week with earnings related, now I get £25. I am very tight at the moment. The rates come in, I had to pay those, then the water rates have to be paid. I've just got in the electricity bill and the gas bill will be in next. I make sure that I pay the bills first before I have food. I've always done that. I have meat on Sundays and that's all. During the week I get fruit and vegetables and they are my main source of food. I might have a couple of slices of bread or some bread rolls from my neighbour and I'll use those. I don't go out. I miss the money and I miss the work. It took me out of the house and I wouldn't need to use any gas or electricity. I don't put anything on at the moment but if it gets any colder I will have to.

I didn't get much redundancy because I left and then went back again. It just paid the rates. Well when I first went on the dole, I went to the Social and I said to the girl, 'How do you expect anybody to manage on that?'. She said, 'I know it isn't much.' I said, 'I live on my own, I have my rent to pay, I have my rates to pay, my electric and my gas, four essentials.' She wrote it all down and she said, 'That leaves you £2.15 to live on.' I said, 'How do you do that?' Well I'm just scratching about. I'm at rock bottom.

Even with a man around there was not a woman, nor a household, that did not notice the absence of her wage. On the whole it was not a case of destitution, but of nagging worry. Young girls were forced into dependence on their parents once again, and newly-married women found themselves faced with large financial commitments that they could not meet on one wage.

Well we'd just got married, and we're buying the house and I didn't know how we were going to cope.

When I was first made redundant and I thought I was never going to get a job, then I felt very guilty and cried, thinking that we weren't going to be able to manage.

Married women with dependent children were confronted with what they always knew. A man's wage is *not* enough to live on.

Well my husband's not on a very good wage. I just do without. I don't buy the things I used to buy. When a woman is working I think you put a lot more into the house. We used to eat a lot of meat. The boys liked steak and chips and things like that. Well they don't get it now. They get mince and they get beefburgers and they get sausages. When I was working I could do it but I can't now, but they don't moan. When I've run out of money and I say right it's beans on toast tonight, they never pull a face. They're not that sort of family that will moan.

I got so fed up by the end. I missed having a bit of money in my purse that I could call my own. When you've only got one man's wage coming in, it's a terrible worry . . . you're always scrimping.

Without exception these women, and men in fact, felt that two wages were necessary to maintain a family household, and where there were no longer two wages being earned, considerable difficulties were experienced. Rather than being concealed the benefits of a woman's wage were very visible. A husband's wage tends to pay for the big regular bills, mortgage, rent, fuel, rates and so on, and women pay for the daily and weekly items, food, clothing and transport. They are *not* insignificant 'extras' and when the income for this expenditure is lost, it has to be found from some other source. It is not always easy for the one wage to meet all of the outgoings as financial commitments are made on the assumption of two regular incomes. Moreover, it is not unusual to find husband and wife both out of work: 'Well it's been difficult. He's been drawing unemployment you know but we've had to dip into his redundancy and we didn't really want to. We've managed to pay our bills, but we've just had to go without things. It's been hard, it's obvious it's going to be.' But women experience much more than financial hardship through the loss of their wage. Not only has a woman's wage secured a higher standard of living for the family, but for women themselves it has brought *financial independence within the family*. The loss of this independence can prompt a personal crisis, commensurate with that which men experience over the loss of their 'breadwinner' status.

For once in my life I feel as though I'm being kept and I've never had that feeling, I've always been very independent, so now I tend to ask his advice on things whereas before I'd have just done it. I've felt it terribly, that loss of independence. I've never been kept by anyone and I think it's terrible. Sometimes he'll say, 'Is that your second packet of cigarettes today?'. Well at one time I'd have said, 'Well who's buying them?' but I can't now. I say, 'Oh well I'm not buying one tomorrow.' You lose your independence.

I don't like being dependent. My husband is very, very good, but it's not my money.

I think I've got a pretty generous husband. If I'd have said I wanted to go to Leeds for a day but couldn't afford it, he would have given me something to go with. But I missed having my own independence. I did miss that a lot, being able to get ready and go where I wanted and do what I wanted and buy what I wanted.

Occupied within the Family?

Because women combine their paid work with their unpaid work in the home, it is easy to construct a female experience of unemployment, as one less problematic than for men. In unemployment, women can busy themselves with domestic routines and the family (which anyway is implicitly neglected by their employment) and therefore do not suffer in the way that men do by a surplus of unstructured time. Given that it appears that half a million women have gone 'off market' since 1977, could it be that women simply respond to redundancy by becoming full-time housewives?

A number of women did in fact have babies after being made redundant. It is difficult to establish a direct causal link with redundancy and motherhood since the women were of an age when they'd have babies anyway. The pressures on women to have children are always enormous: 'We'd been married three years and we had a couple of friends and they'd already had babies and then came the Christmas parties and getting drunk and everything like that and Pete's mum saying, "Oh isn't it time you started a family? What's wrong with you? Don't you love each other or something?".' Job loss can provide that extra incentive: 'You see at Christmas because I didn't have a job, and I thought I wanted to try anyway, and we decided. We'd been married for three years and so we decided to start a family.' Pregnancy and childbirth gives rise to a period in women's lives when they are least rooted in the labour market and are centrally located in the house. Motherhood is a legitimate alternative to working, especially if work had never been enjoyed: 'I've always wanted to finish work, for the last few years I've wanted to pack it in but I just kept going. My husband thought it was a shame it was closing down, but he was glad because he's always wanted me to stop at home. He always has, from us being married. He just likes me being here when he comes home from work.'

Yet, in motherhood women face many of the problems of unemployment: isolation, boredom and the loss of their wage. A baby seems to make the isolation easier: 'I miss my friends. If I hadn't got her and I'd have been at home all day by myself, not had a job, I'd have been bored stiff, but with her I'm alright;' whilst actually being the cause of it: 'Well I went out on Saturday night and that was the first time for a year. My mother babysat. I enjoyed it but I've always been a homebird, I like stopping in, it doesn't bother me but I do miss time on my own now and again. I miss the girls.' Intensified working is not missed: 'I think I have more time now. I definitely don't get bored but I do have more time on my hands, when I can sit down and have a cup of coffee and just relax for a bit, even if it's only 15 minutes, which is one thing I couldn't do at work.' However, the second wage is badly missed. So much so that the decision to give up work doesn't always end at childbirth. These women wavered over their decision not to work and financial need was weighed against practical difficulties. The shift of emphasis in a woman's life does not occur easily or quickly. A lot is given up. In the end women remain at home through lack of any real choice.

I think you need two wages, definitely, but we are managing on one. We've never gone mad, we've always tried to live on so much a week, but with the little one we spend more. There's a place near here and they've been advertising for nightshift vacancies, Monday to Thursday and it's been in my mind to go. But I talked it over with Jim. But I've worked long enough and with him being so small I'll wait. I'll go out when he starts school if I want to.

Well we manage on one wage, we have to. My husband he got made redundant and he's just got a job, so it's been hard for us. You daren't dip into your redundancy because you need it for bills. He was out of work six months. I did think about getting a job when he got made redundant, but then I thought it wasn't really fair of me going out while she was a baby, so I changed my mind. When she goes to school I'll probably get a part-time job, but I wouldn't leave her now. I thought about it when my husband was out of work, but I wouldn't leave her with anybody now. When she's at school, yes.

There's no way I'll go back to work now I've got him because I'd never leave him for someone else to bring up. I want to bring him up on my own, well with my husband of course. I can't see how some mothers can go in for a baby, have it, and then palm it off on someone else to look after until it goes to school. There was one girl where I worked, she had a little boy and three weeks after she had him she handed him over to her mother and was back at work, full time. I think the first couple of years are vital really and they grow up that fast. And I thought well she's not even going to see him grow up. My grandparents brought me up and I can truthfully say there's more of a bond with them than there'll ever be with my parents. I think that's what influenced me in wanting to bring him up myself. I don't even think of getting a job now.

Not all young married women were ready for babies. One 19-year-old explained why she had not opted for motherhood: 'If I'd been a bit older I could have had a baby, but you see I'm 19 and we need some new doors on this place.' For the majority of women this retreat into, and occupation within the family, is not wanted or not possible. Young girls all too easily get sucked into the domestic work of the family:

I do all the jobs that a housewife would do. I do most of the housework and the shopping and the cooking. I sometimes do the washing, but she doesn't really trust me with that. My mother works until five o'clock, so when she comes home she likes to relax.

I find it very depressing and I have these phases where I burst out into tears and everything because I get right upset about not working. Me mum doesn't help. She gives me work to do around the house. I suppose it does help her because she goes out at eight o'clock so it does help her a lot if when she comes home she has nothing to do.

Work at least provides an escape from the domestic routine, which is all too ready to absorb them. It provides money and freedom and some kind of life outside of the family: 'I miss the people. Work is company, it's meeting people. When I've been working I've quite enjoyed it but when I'm out of work it's not very nice. When you're working at least I know that I've got some money of my own to spend.'

Most women cannot afford *not* to be wage earners, nor would they want to be fully occupied with the family. Redundancy is however an opportunity to have a 'rest'. It is not something that would have been chosen, but in the event of it happening, redundancy is a release from an exhausting working life, in the factory and in the home:

Well to bring that money home you had to work like heck for it and sometimes you didn't dare go to the toilet because every single minute counted. You daren't otherwise the minutes ticked away and that was the worst thing, because in so many minutes you had to do so many trousers . . . it knocked your numbers down and then you had to work to try and get them up again. Even then you couldn't really go too mad because I cut a few chunks out of my fingers now and again. It used to be terrible. Not very much got done because as soon as I came in I'd cook a meal, but that was my lot. I just used to sit in front of the fire. I must admit I did like being off work.

I don't know how I did it. I used to have a routine. Mondays I used to come home and do upstairs, Tuesdays I did down here, Wednesdays I washed. I did my dad's washing as well and I did his bungalow out on Friday nights. Well I still do that. But then I did it all after I'd finished work. I did the shopping on Wednesdays, it's late night then. I still do that, but I haven't got a routine at all now. I've gone to pot!

Redundancy pay *does* soften the blow and, given the pressure of their lives, it is impossible for women not to have an ambivalent response to job loss.[7] In the early weeks many cupboards were cleared out, rooms redecorated and curtains washed:

Being at home was nice to start with. It was nice because I was able to pick up all what I hadn't done, or what I'd have to fit in between working. Things like having a good clear out and emptying cupboards. All the things you put off.

I had plenty to do at first. I decorated all upstairs.

I'd been promising to decorate the place and this year I got it done. I've decorated inside and out. I've started tiling the floor now.

Women *do* occupy themselves with the household and more readily than men can. Women already have a place there and men do not. But in the longer term, it is not an alternative to employment. They miss their wage:

It was actually a bit of a break at the time, a welcome break. It's when the money runs out that you feel it. Naturally I thought it was a bit hard, you get used to going out to work and having that independence and that money. You don't feel it so much at first because the redundancy carries you over for a certain period. When you've caught up with things at home, that's when it begins to tell. It's the money, prices still keep going up and bills have to be met.

Moreover, they are essentially, working women. Once the pressure eased, household jobs were done, all the problems of surplus unstructured time are experienced by women: 'You don't miss it straight away you see, you've got your redundancy money . . . Then I got everything done and then I got bored. I couldn't stop all day long in the house. I wouldn't like to spend all day in the house clearing up, every day forever.' Although women never have enough time, the *quality* of that time matters: 'I got bored but now that I'm working again I realise that I shouldn't have been really. But you miss people. You sort of tend to live in your own little world.' The previous *pace* of life is missed. At least it was a life. Unemployment can appear to be the end of everything:

> I've been doing a lot of knitting to pass the time. You get up in the morning, give them their breakfast, then you decide you're going to start your housework, you know you've got no need to rush it, so you linger, you do a bit more than you usually do. You take your time going to the shops, probably meet up with the neighbours that you haven't seen for years and stop and have a chinwag with them. Come home, do the tea for the men coming in. I'd rather be rushed off my feet. When I was working I used to come home, dash to the shops, a quick flip round the shops, come home start the tea, flash round with the hoover and duster. I'd dash up and have a bath and be off somewhere for the evening. Now I seem to be missing out on everything. When you've worked all your life, and you come to this point, you just feel as if your life's come to a standstill.

Changing Roles?

Men cope with unemployment in a similar way to women, in that they try to occupy themselves more in the home. Sometimes with housework, to the extent that they threaten to displace their wives, but more usually with house repairs, decorating and DIY. The men's crisis is often because they do *not* have any real relation to the domestic routine. Being at home reinforces their demoralisation: 'I'd go to the Job Centre, come home, do nothing much. I lost interest in a lot of things. I didn't do anything around the house I just hated it, it was degrading, it was a nightmare. I got the feeling that I was never going to work again.'

Men did enjoy aspects of being at home more, having time with their children, even the luxury of watching television during the day. The daily grind of work was not missed by men either but the structure and the social relations it created were. Moreover, unemployed men in the home are invading a wife's terrain. Many women found this loss of space and natural order difficult to bear. It is a recipe for domestic tension:

> I quite enjoyed having him at home at first but then I got resentful, even though I knew the circumstances. I was going out to work, and doing the housework and he stayed at home doing nothing. He was always there, do you know what I mean?

> He was absolutely bored stiff. I could find something to do, clean drawers out or something, but he couldn't. I'd rather him go to work and his tea's ready when he comes home, so you're in a routine of your own, but when they're at home you just can't get anything done. You get used to having the house to yourself during the day.

Women's unemployment does not cause the same problem. It can actually enhance men's domestic lives.

> Well everything's done now when he gets in. He knows his meals will be ready on time, and he can just sit down for the night.

> Well my husband isn't very fond of housework and doesn't like getting his own meals ready and things like that. I think he liked the money coming in, but now he also likes the fact that his meals are ready when he comes in.

Although men and women used the home to cope with the surplus of time created by unemployment, it cannot have any lasting effect on the division of labour between men and women within the home. Unemployment is structured as a temporary phenomenon and not one that can and ought to be adjusted to. Restructuring cannot take place because men are actively job seeking. In many instances unemployment for men does assume a sort of permanence, as more and more men are becoming long-term unemployed. Yet it is a permanent state of suspension. It cannot be the basis for long-term change or new initiatives. The problem for men with being at home during unemployment was not only to do with having surplus unstructured time. Rather it is a daily confrontation with the fact that they are not doing what men are supposed to do; not simply to work, but to be the breadwinners. The idea that men are the breadwinners remains a very potent one, shared by many women:

> I think it's much worse for a man to be made redundant than a woman. I think women have got another interest, there is the home isn't there, and I don't think men are the same. Although I would strongly fight against this myself, to belittle a man because he wasn't working, there's an awful lot of women that would. There's more stigma attached to a man, after all he's the breadwinner and no matter how hard a woman works, you need that man's wage coming in. And I think for a man to lose that he's lost all his dignity.

> I would imagine it's degrading for a man, because I don't believe in this women's lib, you know. I think the man should be the man. I think a woman should have a bit of independence but I think it's important for the man to think he's the breadwinner. For a man to be out of work and his wife working must be terrible. I think it would affect a man's mind more than a woman.

The persistence of the idea that men are the breadwinners is of course rooted in some material fact. Men *do* earn more than women and whilst that is the case, the larger wage is the most significant one. In reality many women know that men's capacity to be the breadwinner is only as secure as their job. Male unemployment means that a woman's wage has never been more significant: 'Last year was a terrible year for us. He was without work for four months and there was only my wage coming in, so, it was a tightrope, we did make ends meet but that was about all. If I hadn't have been working, we just couldn't have managed. Then he got a very low-paid job, but then I was made redundant. . . .' Preserving men as the breadwinners, means preserving the male ego:

> I think it's worse for men. Men get very demoralised. When I first left school, because I'd been going out with my husband over five years before we got married, I got a job straight away. I wasn't out of a job, I was even working when I was at school. I used to do Saturday jobs and evening jobs. When he first left school he couldn't find a job. We used to go out and I had all the money and he didn't have any, so if we wanted to go to the pictures or anything, I always used to pay for him and he didn't like it at all. We did actually split up for a couple of months because of it. When he got his apprenticeship, he came back, well he didn't actually go for good, we still kept seeing each other but he wouldn't go out with me because he knew I would be paying for everything and he didn't like that one little bit. I think men, especially if they're married, feel very belittled. But as soon as he got a job that was it. He wasn't very pleased when I worked at Roger Firth and I was bringing in more than him. He felt threatened. But I told him I wasn't going round telling everybody I earned more than him and we pooled our money together anyway. It wasn't as if we'd leave ourselves so much out of our wage, so that I'd have at the end of the week £15 to spend and he'd only got £5, we pooled it together. He came round in the end.

It has been women's employment rather than men's unemployment that has effected change in the sexual division of labour and women's lives. Although it is clear that capitalist waged labour exploits gender divisions, rather than freeing women from them, nevertheless women's entry into paid work has been a major force for change. Women have had to enter paid work, grappling with the contradictory tensions of the material fact of their employment and the ill-defined parameters of femininity. One effect has been to enlarge the boundaries of 'women's role' further and faster than for men. Through their employment, the role of women has been radically disturbed, whereas change for men has been slower and uneven. Women are now represented as having a 'dual role' and femininity can span, albeit uneasily, the family *and* employment. In their dual role the dilemmas of femininity are resolved, women can have children, be responsible for household organisation and through their wage earning contribute to family income. It is not an easy one and every woman suffers at some stage in her life from the conflict implicit in her feminine role. The very concept of dual role implies a reconciliation of the two spheres of a woman's life, when in fact it is an ill-defined and tortuous mix. But women have never been clearer about their need and right to work:

Married women need to work just as much as anyone else.

If all the married women stopped working, I don't know what would happen to this country.

No woman works for pin money. I mean the men, none of them are over-generous with their money are they? Let's face it. I mean not like a woman. She goes to work and she brings all her wage packet home and most of it goes in the house or on the kids.

They couldn't run this country without married women anyway. I think women are much better workers than men. Men wouldn't do the jobs that we do. Even youngsters wouldn't do that job I did at Roger Firth because it was monotonous. I think it's absolutely necessary that women work, both for industry and for the home. To keep the home going. We're going to have a lot lower standard of living if women don't work. I don't believe in women leaving young children. I'm all for places that will do part time and I'm all for this scheme, so that when women do return to work they don't lose anything by it.

But I think a woman has as much right to go out to work as a man has, she has only one life and it's very tiring to be in four walls all day. Women should have the independence of knowing 'well I've earned that'. I don't think a man should turn round and say, 'Well I've married you and I'll keep you' and expect you to kowtow to everything they want. No, I believe that women should have a life of their own.

Out-of-work women experience many of the problems that men experience. Women do still have household labour, but they are used to *combining* it with paid employment. The period women spend at home as full-time housewives is a very specific one. It is the period in which they care for preschool children. Otherwise, women, like men, derive a crucial sense of themselves through the social relations of work. Without work they are not only isolated, they are separated from what appears to be the mainstream of life.

Unemployment throws masculinity into crisis, because it is still centred on work and wage earning. Men still undertake very little childcare and very little housework, and unemployment will not change that, not simply because of it being a temporary situation, but because of men's resistance to domestic involvement. Even in situations where it would make financial sense for a woman to work, to become the breadwinner in the face of a husband's long-term unemployment, there is an opposition to that kind of 'role reversal'. 'Well I'd like that, but he wouldn't!'

Men's involvement with their children can also be insubstantial. Yet how can they become carers when they need women's care themselves?

He looks after her but, I know it sounds funny to say it, but I've always got the impression that he's frightened, deep down he doesn't know how to cope. I get that impression from him, I always have done, since she was little, when I first brought her home. He'd be all over her, round her, but he'd be nervous about holding her. I don't think he really knows what to do. He'll put her to bed and he'll go up and read her a story. He takes her swimming. When it comes down to it, basically I've had to be the one that's seen to her because he's a person who needs somebody himself. . . .

And perhaps that is the point. Domestic labour is more than

simply looking after the house and children, it is the servicing of men. How can men participate in their own servicing? If men genuinely shared in the domestic work of the household, the very fabric of the relationship between men and women would be transformed.

Women who have returned to work after a period of being at home are, paradoxically, those least rooted in an ideology of femininity. They have had marriage, kids and full-time domesticity and, as they return to work, they claim back a bit of themselves. They have got the kids off their hands, they have financial independence, they are social beings once more. They are mature women who have learned a few things, and it is their time. Redundancy and unemployment comes hard. Whatever the nature of their exploitation at work, wage labour has purchased women a measure of emancipation. The family cannot make sense of their unemployment, because work has been for women, a route out of the family. They are, consequently, workers without work. 'I felt as if I'd been thrown on the scrap heap, nobody wanted to know, nobody's bothered.'

In a contracting labour market it is particularly difficult for older women to find work, and to them the family offers no sop to this painful process.

There's a lot to be said for working, I think it keeps you young. I think you pay too much attention to your small ailments when you're at home. I was never one for having time off work and I would get up even if I didn't feel very well and think it would go off when I got to work, and it did. But I think if you're at home you think 'oh I don't feel at all good' and you give in to it. I think working with young people makes you feel young. I think I've aged since I finished work. I've got very weepy. I miss people and responsibility.

The last time I went for a job and she said, 'We'll let you know', I said, 'For God's sake tell people straight. Why don't you tell us we're too old?' You feel as if you're ready for dying. I can't believe it. It's lonely, I even went after the toilet job in town, the

119

public toilets. I've got my name down everywhere. It's depressing. I have many a weep, I can't help it. You just can't believe it's come to this. This has been the hardest time of my life. I mean I've been on strikes in Leeds and that, but I knew we'd get back to work. It's never been like this.

6
Back to the Home?

What emerges from these women's accounts is the extraordinary attachment women have to their paid employment. Moreover this is not simply a question of financial need, for women derive satisfaction and status from their work. This should not be surprising but it is. Familial ideology has been very successful in marginalising women's work, even to women themselves, and, paradoxically, it is often only on the occasion of the loss of that work that its full significance becomes apparent.

What is clear is that the impact of unemployment on women can no more be understood solely within explanations of women's familial role, any more than men's unemployment can be understood solely in terms of their economic role. For men, work is an integral part of their daily, social relations *as men*, and job loss affects them as men, not simply as waged labour. It may be that, because women still have an ongoing role within the family, unemployment and the ensuing confinement to the household does not pitch them into crisis in the way it may do for men. Unemployment for women is not a crisis of gender identity and women's domestic role can offer ways of making sense of job loss. As has been seen, some women from Roger Firth *enlarged* the domestic role, either by spending more time on housework or, exceptionally, by having babies. Yet within the range of experiences indicated in this book, shared experiences have also emerged. As for men, unemployment for women means financial hardship, isolation and depression. Additionally however, unemployment for women is often experienced as a crisis of autonomy, as a loss of independence, and here women's domestic role is no compensation. On the contrary, work for women has been their *route out* of domestic and financial dependence. Consequently, the family may soften the blow of job loss, but in the end the family appears to be the trap.

This book has concentrated on the experiences of a relatively small number of women. Yet redundancy, job loss and unemployment for women are now frequent occurrences and although there will inevitably be differences arising from the conditions of local labour markets and local skills, there is no reason to suppose that the core experience radically differs. There are common problems facing women in the 1980s. The issues of unemployment, recession and contracting job markets go beyond local case studies, indeed go far beyond being simply 'women's issues', and it is worth putting the Harrogate and Castleford studies into a broader and political context.

Although the numbers of unemployed women have been increasing rapidly there has been a refusal to recognise female unemployment as being comparable with male unemployment. Rather, it is constructed as being different for women, in that it is not the same condition of hardship, either economically or emotionally, because women, it is assumed, are supported by the family and occupied within it. Insofar as there is any official identification of a problem in relation to women, it remains, as Sinfield has argued, concerned with women's *employment* and the implicit neglect of family, not with their unemployment (Sinfield, 1981, p. 86). Consequently, the problems associated with permanently high rates of unemployment, continue to be associated with *male* unemployment. This book has questioned some of those assumptions.

What are the causes of women's unemployment? Are women more vulnerable to job loss than men? What is the effect of unemployment on women? How does it compare with men's experiences? In a situation of job shortage, are women returning to the home? What impact are high levels of unemployment having on women's jobs and job opportunities.

In the asking of those questions, it has become clear that female unemployment is a very real problem in which women experience economic and personal hardships similar to men. Yet, whilst high unemployment *is* discouraging some women from seeking work, there is no real question of women 'returning' to the home or being supported by the family. The conditions of recession, inflation, the devaluation of the male wage and, above all, male unemployment, have *increased* the pressure on women to work. Unemployment for women is an enforced period of worklessness, but it is also one aspect of a deteriorating labour market situation. The contraction of the female labour market is forcing women to accept increasingly exploitative forms of work. Often part-time work, temporary work and homework, at very low rates of pay, are all that is available. What is happening, is not that the family is supporting women in recession, but that it is concealing the difficulties they face.

Unemployment and Job Loss

Since the Second World War, successive governments in Britain, both Labour and Conservative, have been committed to the principle of full employment; a commitment rooted in political and democratic principles, as well as Keynesian economic theory, that a return to the unemployment levels of the 1930s would be irreconcilable with the ideals of post-war British social democracy. Full employment was made possible by steady economic growth in Britain, sustained through the late 1950s and 1960s, which kept unemployment at very low levels: 2 percent or approximately 400,000 people. The commitment to full employment was actually a commitment to full *male* employment, but economic expansion and especially the growth of the service sector in the post-war period drew more and more women into the labour force, so that by 1970 the number of economically-active women has virtually doubled from pre-war levels, whilst the number of male workers remained stable. This very long-term trend in the post-war period for the number of women at work to grow has been sustained despite cyclical recession. By 1977, the economic activity rate for women peaked to a point higher than at any other time since the early Industrial Revolution and higher than any other European country.

123

Unemployment amongst men and women started to increase in the early 1970s but with numbers held at approximately one million. In the 'mini-boom' of 1974 these figures even went down, but from 1979 unemployment figures have increased rapidly, with women becoming unemployed at a rate much faster than men (EOC, 1981, p. 72). Job loss and unemployment amongst women only rapidly accelerated from the late 1970s onwards, whereas male unemployment had started to increase far sooner. It appears that women's employment levels were maintained longer by the continued availability of work for women in the service sector, especially part-time work (Brueghal, 1979; Elias and Main, 1982). But the very reasons for that early protection are now placing women in an acutely vulnerable position. Women do not have the same jobs as men, rather, they are segregated and concentrated in a narrow range of industries and occupations (Hakim, 1979). Moreover, women have, on the whole, been employed in services, in labour-intensive jobs and often in under-capitalised and less stable sectors of the economy (Barron and Norris, 1976; Braverman, 1974; Weir and McIntosh, 1982). In recession many of these jobs have been lost.

Insofar as they are located in the unstable secondary sector, women's jobs are the most prone to increased competition and economic collapse, but, perhaps most significantly, recession has forced a series of cost-saving and labour-saving strategies and many industries which have employed large numbers of women have been both reorganising their labour process and restructuring the enterprise. In recession women's jobs are also threatened by reorganisation, new technology and relocation.

Office work, shop work, assembly and packaging account for a large proportion of female occupations (Huws, 1982), and it is these jobs which are now being reorganised on the principles of scientific management and transformed by the introduction of micro-technology. New technology, in particular, diminishes the cost advantage of women's cheaper labour, increases productivity, and is likely to cause *massive* and permanent job losses amongst women (Barker and Downing, 1980; Hines and Searle, 1979; Huws, 1982). The full effects of such technological change are yet

124

to be seen, but at the moment there is little indication that women will find alternative employment in those areas where new technology is *creating* employment. The *number* of jobs being created, relative to the numbers lost, is insignificant because the technology is being introduced in a period of recession rather than expansion. Insofar as new technology is creating more skilled, technical jobs, women do not have access to them. Women still have not been able to broaden their education and training opportunities. Where unskilled, labour-intensive work for women is maintained, or even created by new technology, there is now evidence that such jobs are being relocated to the Third World.

Such relocation of labour-intensive production to low-wage economies is now a structural feature of developed Western economies and multi-national corporations (Froebal *et al.*, 1979). It amounts to a kind of international 'putting out' system (Elson and Pearson, 1981, p. 88). Third World countries can provide a very favourable climate – free trade zones and few, if any, workers' employment rights – to secure both cheap labour and a degree of control over labour, not possible in the UK (Elson and Pearson, p. 90). Such relocation of production can restore the profitability of many companies but it means irretrievable job loss in the UK. This solution to recession has already been resorted to by clothing and textiles manufacturers. Now, as jobs are created by the micro-electronic industry, many jobs for women will not be found in the UK but in the Far East where female labour is more exploitable (Grossman, 1979).

In public and private services the job situation is less clear. Cutbacks in government spending on public services has meant the loss of many women's jobs, but at the same time privatisation and the continued provision of private services has maintained some employment for women. Cleaning floors, cooking school meals and looking after old people and children, are the kinds of jobs which women do and, although such work has been reorganised and intensified, on the whole it is little affected by technology.

In total, however, women's jobs do appear very vulnerable. The fear that whole areas of women's employment are to be subjected to the kind of 'wholesale elimination' that some traditionally male industries have had to face, mining, railways and docks, for example (Brueghal, p. 20), is well grounded. If this does happen women will have nowhere else to go. Contraction in those areas of the economy which employ women means that women's jobs are disproportionately devastated. Rising female unemployment, combined with the drop in the economic activity rate for women (DOE, April 1981), seems to confirm that women are being discouraged from seeking work and pressured into remaining at home.

The Politics of Recession

High levels of unemployment have been caused by world-wide economic recession. In the UK they have been exacerbated by low productivity, high inflation and the failure to be competitive on foreign markets. Since 1979, the recession has been managed by the Thatcher Government's monetarist policies. As essentially deflationary policies they have undoubtedly contributed to rising unemployment levels. Managed within a theory of monetarism, the recession has been constructed and understood within a philosophy of radical conservatism, in which unemployment has been represented as an inevitable and unavoidable precondition for economic recovery. The slide into this view of unemployment is a move away from Keynesian economic theory which holds that unemployment levels can be controlled. Moreover it is a radical break with the social-democratic ideals of the post-war consensus and from any commitment to either full employment or equal opportunities for women.

A high rate of job loss and unemployment amongst women, combined with the departure from any official concern or commitment to equal opportunities, has led to extensive fears that the Tory government is seeking to return women to the home as a solution to unemployment (CIS, 1980). At no stage has there been any *stated* government policy on the position of women at work, and there has been no concerted government attack on women, in the way that there has been on trade union organisation, for example, but individual government ministers have not been slow in articulating their opposition to women working, and recent revelations in the press that Margaret Thatcher has set up a special policy group to consider ways of encouraging women not to work, and to review the position of the Equal Opportunities Commission, has struck a chill wind in the hearts and minds of many. Although there is no evidence that women can 'save' men from unemployment in this way (Rubery and Tarling, 1982), there is certainly gathering support for the idea that women remaining at home could ease the pressure on jobs.

To date, it is the *effects* of monetarist policies which have had greater implications for women than ideological statements. It has already been argued that such policies have worsened the state of economic decline in recession in the UK generally, but additionally, during the last four years, there have been massive cutbacks in government spending on welfare provision. Cutbacks in education, health and social services have affected women as public services employees and as consumers of those services. The government has sought ways of reducing its spending and money flow believing it to be inflationary. In doing so they have caused job losses amongst women *and* they have sought to shift the onus of responsibility for the provision of welfare services on to the family and, implicitly, on to women. The attempt to cut spending and to relocate welfare provision within the family, has taken place within a clear set of ideological manoeuvres. Welfare is being cut, not because the government is too mean to meet that provision but because its rightful place is within the caring bosom of the family. But whose bosom?

Let us ignore for the moment that the Welfare State was established precisely because the family could not meet its own immediate needs, let alone care for the sick and elderly, and consider who will provide this 'traditional' family care. Men, we know, are wage earners, so they are not able to and women – well, so are they. The family can no more provide total care and welfare for its members now, than it could prior to the Welfare State. In

127

fact, the family is now worse off than it was in 1960 (Study Commission on the Family, 1983). Government policies over the last fours years have, ironically, contributed to the need for women to work. Yet they have also sought to diminish any claim that women have either to the right to work or the right for those public services which facilitate the combining of family responsibility with wage earning.

Women, Work and the Family

The notion that women could be 'restored' to the home in any simple and unproblematic way can only be constructed because of the conditions under which women have entered paid work in the first instance. Despite the dramatic increase in the number of women, and especially married women, in employment, women have continued to be deemed responsible for domestic labour in the home and the care of children, husbands and often other relatives as well. This combination of work and family was represented in the idea that women have a 'dual role' (Myrdal and Klein, 1956). Although it was a very radical idea at the time in that it made a claim for the right for women to work, it does not challenge the sexual division of labour between men and women, and the allocation of domestic labour to women; rather it says that women can do both.

It is now clear that the ongoing location of women within the family and the domestic situation, has both practically confined women's employment opportunities and ideologically allowed for the marginalisation of women's work. Women's entry into paid work has occurred within the structural confines of the sexual division of labour, and, despite the reality of women's employment and a real dependence on their wage-earning capacity, it has been possible to maintain an ambiguity about where women actually 'belong'.

There have in fact been enormous structural changes, both within the economy and within the family, that make it extremely unlikely that easy reversals can take place. In common with other

128

industrialised countries, the service sector is now a significant part of the UK economy and more people are employed in services than in any other sector. At the same time that expansion of the service sector has been premised on the availability of female labour upon which it is heavily dependent. Neither recession nor monetarist policies are likely to reverse such long-term economic trends. At the same time there have also been important structural changes within the family. There has been a decrease in family size and a reduction in the child-bearing period, so that both the number of dependent children in the family and the period for which they are dependent, has been considerably reduced. The effects of these changes have meaning for both men and women. It is now the case that only 18 percent of all men in the labour force are the sole breadwinners in their family (CSO, 1981). At the same time an increasing proportion of single-parent families are headed by women. An increasing number of women with dependent children are returning to work, and now one in seven earn as much, if not more, than their husbands (EOC, 1981a, pp. 80–1). The income which a woman contributes to the family household often means the difference between poverty and a reasonable standard of living. Without it, one in three families would be living beneath the official poverty line (Royal Commission on the Distribution of Income and Wealth, 1978). What has taken place since the war has been a process which Braverman called the 'capitalisation' of the family (1974, pp. 281–3). Women have been drawn into the cash nexus which has created a mutually-interacting need of an economy dependent on women's labour in significant sectors, and of a family household now dependent on a woman's wage. What we are seeing in recession, precisely because of this mutual interaction, is an ever-increasing need to exploit women's labour and women being forced into an increased acceptance of the worst kind of jobs.

While it may be that more women are making up a 'silent reserve' who have been discouraged from seeking work in recession, on the whole the conditions of recession are such that it places increasing pressure on women to find work. Recession, inflation and high levels of unemployment devalue the male wage, interrupt men's capacity to work at all and exposes the material fallacy of the male wage as a family breadwinner's wage. If women are being affected by unemployment, there is no evidence that this is in any way diminishing their attachment to work.

Monetarism in the Labour Market

In the first four years of its administration the Thatcher government sought to 'free' the labour market. Their policies are derived from neo-classicist economic theory which considers that the labour market and the price of labour has to find its 'floor'. Consequently, the government regards trade union action and legislation securing guaranteed minimum wages as preventing the 'natural' price of labour emerging. In their view one cause of unemployment has been that wages have been too high and employment can only be sustained through lower wages and more 'flexible' employment conditions. Monetarist economic theory put into practice what amounts to a major political offensive. Wages councils and minimum wage agreements are being abolished and employment protection and trade union powers restricted.

These policies have especially serious implications for women. Wage levels are not set through market forces, but rather through the expectation of a certain standard of living and through trade union organisation. Women have always been weakly organised within trade unions and it is still possible to pay women a wage that does not meet their full living costs (Rubery and Tarling, 1981). Amendments to the Employment Protection Act (1980) have placed more women outside of its scope and, even though some employers do not feel obliged to observe even minimum wage regulations (Williams, 1972), for many women the removal of minimum wage guarantees will remove the *only* wage protection that they have.

Fears that women could be dispatched back into the home on a scale comparable to that which occurred in the late nineteenth century, are rooted both in the evident increase of job loss amongst women, and government policies which are contributing both to job loss and creating a climate hostile to women working. Yet such government intervention in the labour market is making it possible to cheapen women's labour further and, as such, to help contribute to the conditions where women are a preferred source of labour. Their labour is cheaper than men's. Government policies are not anti-feminist in the explicit way that occurred in the 1930s when women's employment was represented as a partial *cause* of recession and unemployment, and the expulsion of women from the labour market was actively sought (Humphries, 1976). Monetarism has many prongs and both needs women in the home, taking on the burden of care in order to reduce public spending, and needs women in the labour market to effect a downward pressure on wages.

The Growth of Part-time Work

The 1981 Census of Employment indicates that between 1978 and 1981 there was an increase of a quarter of a million jobs in the service sector, but they were almost entirely part-time jobs and almost entirely occupied by women. Although there has been some continued growth during the recession, in miscellaneous services and personal services, for example, this alone cannot account for the growth in part-time work. What has also occurred, and is still taking place, is a fundamental restructuring of the economy through the reorganisation of work and the introduction of new technology. Where job growth is arising it is not so much from expansion as from an extensive job carve up. This appears to be borne out by the fact that the numbers of hours worked by part-timers have reduced, with more part-timers than ever working between 8–16 hours a week (Robinson, 1982). This apparent growth of employment for women has to be seen in the context of overall job loss – that is the loss of full-time jobs. It was in the service sector that the enormous expansion of part-time work for women first took place, to *attract* women into employment, but now part-time work organisation is one strategy to effect a further

131

cheapening of labour costs and a greater flexibility of labour. We are seeing a growth of jobs arising from an increasing casualisation of work; full-time jobs are becoming part time and permanent jobs are becoming temporary.

Part-time Work and Women

Part-time work has always been characterised by low pay, unskilled work, job insecurity and little or no promotion prospects (Hurstfield, 1978). It has been a form of organising work that enables employers to have flexibility to extend or shorten the working day according to the peaks and troughs of demand. Women have been attracted to part-time work because that flexibility of time enables them to cope with wage earning *and* their unpaid work in the home. It is very difficult for women to combine childcare and household organisation with full-time work. Women do so, often under enormous personal pressure (Cooper and Davidson, 1982), often needing to enlist outside help, either paid help (Rapoport and Rapoport, 1971) or, as is more usually the case for working-class women, other female relatives (Chaney, 1981). Women may now be sharing with men the responsibility of wage earning, but there is little sign of men taking on their share of domestic responsibility.

For this reason part-time work is the work of married women and particularly women with children. Part-time hours are not necessarily arranged to suit married women with children. Part-time shifts, evening shifts, split shifts and so on, can be very inconvenient and are organised around the requirements of the industry and enterprise, rather than women (Liff, 1981). It is the provision of *reduced* working hours which attracts women to part-time working and which makes women's dual role – or dual burden – possible.

The cost of part-time working to women has been enormous. In the first place, it has made it *possible* for women to be wage earners and domestic labourers without there having been any real redistribution of domestic work between men and women. As a result, women have remained defined in terms of the domestic and through this are structured as a secondary, marginal and *subordinate* labour force. Part-time work is not just the work of married women, it is specifically the work of women *returning* to the labour market after a period of being at home with small children (Elias and Main, 1982). But because most part-time work is only available in low-skilled, low-paid jobs, women's need for reduced working hours confines them to such work and effectively deskills them. There is often a gross mismatch between women's skills and their part-time work. Elias and Main found in the evidence from the National Training Survey that, 'one part-timer in 25 with a teaching qualification is in the low-skilled catering or cleaning occupations, as is one part-timer in 12 with nursing qualifications' (1982, p. 4). It is very difficult to find part-time work in more skilled, responsible and better-paid occupations. In the civil service for example, 87 percent of all part-timers are in the clerical grade (EOC, 1981a), or where it is available, in teaching for example, it forms a sub-category of labour within the profession with no security of employment or promotion. There is invariably very little choice about part-time working, and women often find it difficult to get out of. As children grow older many women want full-time work but the move from part-time working to full time can be as difficult as re-entry into the labour market. Women who pressingly need a full-time wage have sometimes to resort to taking two part-time jobs.

The vulnerability of women in part-time work arises because they often do not have the employment rights and protection of full-time workers. Part-timers do not necessarily have to be paid the same rate as full-timers and this is reflected in the 1981 hourly earnings of part-timers which have deteriorated to 86 percent of full-time rates (Robinson, 1982), and even then there is a tendency to overestimate part-time average earnings because the lowest paid are left out of these figures altogether (Hurstfield, 1980). Some part-timers will have job protection under the Employment Protection Act, provided they work sufficient hours in a week and have long enough service records to establish continuous employment. But it is the very nature of part-time work that it is erratic and short term, and that both hours and continuity are

133

difficult to maintain. Indeed it is a common strategy of some employers to make sure that their part-time employees do not qualify for job protection under the Act. As many as 29 percent of part-timers are not covered by the Employment Protection Act because their weekly earnings are below the National Insurance threshold of £23 a week. Many part-timers will have no entitlement to a pension, sick pay, holiday pay, maternity pay, bonus premiums and, in the event of redundancy, redundancy pay. As unprotected labour, part-time workers are very attractive to employers, cheaper to employ and cheaper to dismiss.

Approximately four million women now work part time. Yet the growth in part-time work really reflects a more general situation. Women are continuing to find work because women are, on the whole, more flexible than men. That is to say, women will work inconvenient, unsocial hours, in unskilled, low-status jobs for very little pay. On the whole women are more vulnerable than men to poor working conditions because they do not have men's background of skill, trade unionism, the male wage and are also often disenfranchised from subsistence-level Social Security provision. So a job is a job. It must be said that where men do attempt to find work in what is essentially 'women's work' they are often discriminated against by employers (House of Lords, 1982, p. 59), and for such low-paid work women are clearly a preferred source of labour. Official statistics of employment neither measure the personal cost to women in being forced into this kind of work, nor the erosion of employment conditions that is taking place. Yet the women who appear in the case study behind this book nearly all illustrate how they were forced into work that they would not previously have considered and they are being deskilled by recession and job shortage. Women who had been highly skilled and relatively well paid (for women in manual occupations), found themselves cleaning in hotels, hospitals and other people's houses, for just over a pound an hour, often for a few hours a day, on a temporary contract with no job security.

Women are suffering badly from job loss, as can be measured by the increase in both the *rate* at which women are becoming unemployed, and the *duration* of their unemployment. Yet at the same time there is evidence that women are continuing to find alternative work and more easily than men. In some regions where male employment has been decimated by large-scale closures and redundancies, this has created a 'feminisation' of the labour force (Williams, 1982).[8] There is every reason to suppose that this trend will continue. The only significant job growth forecasted is in low-grade, part-time employment, and women continue to be a preferred labour supply for this kind of work. Their subordinate position within the family reaffirms and extends the possibilities of exploiting women at work.

7
What is to be Done?

What the women from Roger Firth make clear is that women are continuing to seek paid employment and are finding it, but under ever worsening conditions. Women are finding work not simply because they are cheaper to employ than men but also because of their extraordinary flexibility. Employers are getting away with appalling practices, and especially by manipulating pay and part-time hours in order to reduce women's wages further. The equal pay and anti-discrimination legislation of the 1970s has always been limited in its scope, but in the 1980s it is becoming almost irrelevant. Formal equality is not the point. It is starkly apparent that employers are fully exploiting the sexual division of labour within the family. They are aided and abetted by Tory government policies and by men, who as trade unionists and husbands, often short-sightedly seek to preserve a status quo that is comforting to their masculinity. It is a missed opportunity for radicalism and unity and again has ramifications that go far beyond the Harrogate and Castleford study. The fundamental problem facing women in employment is not that they do not have equal opportunities, but that *they have too much domestic labour* and *they do not have a form of collective organisation which is representative of their interests.*

Strategies for the Eighties

In the sphere of women's employment, the issues are the same as ever. Women still need to earn a decent, living wage; to have access to training and skilled, well-paid jobs; to have more flexible working conditions and shorter hours; and need men to take responsibility for their share of childcare and domestic labour. The issues of the sixties and seventies are still the issues for the eighties, but the economic and political climate in which they are to be confronted is a very different one. The programme for equal opportunities for women that took place in the 1970s occurred within the context of an economy, which although declining, still offered employment opportunities and a political environment of social democratic consensus, which embraced the idea of women's formal equality with men. It has already been argued in the previous chapter that economic recession and rising unemployment is being politically managed in the 1980s by a radical conservatism which has broken from any commitment to maintaining either employment levels or equal opportunities. This means not just that the economic and political climate in Britain in the 1980s is less receptive to women's demands, but that those demands have themselves to embody and tackle changed circumstances. High levels of unemployment are forecasted to persist well up to 1990, if not beyond (University of Warwick Institute of Employment Research, 1982). Women's needs for, and in, employment have to be reconciled with the fact that there are millions of men and women who are, long term, without work. High unemployment increases poverty and sharpens inequality. The state system of Unemployment Benefit is hopelessly inadequate and still based on the provision established by Beveridge in the immediate post-war period. The ethos of this was a stop-gap provision, conceived within the context of full male employment, not structural unemployment. It is impossible to think about what has to be done about women at work without thinking about what has to be done to bring about a redistribution of work and a redistribution of income. Not that women should subjugate their interests to the more burning issues of the day, but that it is the *only* way that women are going to achieve real economic independence.

The Problem with Equal Opportunities

In the post-war period in Britain, economic growth, progress and equal opportunity were inextricably linked with an ideology of 'progressivism' (Finn *et al.*, 1977, p. 176). The problems of inequality and poverty were to be overcome through material growth. Specifically, it would provide women with the opportunities for employment, which in turn would gradually erode those elements of discrimination against women which remained rooted in traditional, and misplaced, anti-feminist attitudes. Legislation for equal opportunities was rooted in this idealism of 'progressivism', even though, in fact, the Equal Pay Act and Anti-Discrimination Act (1975) had to be fought for tooth and nail and implementation was delayed for five years. This legislation provided for women's formal equality with men, and legislative redress to overcome those remaining elements of discrimination which persisted in the age of enlightenment. Although a belated response to the wider changes that had been taking place in the economy, the family and women's lives, the legislation did mark an official commitment to equal opportunities for women. It provided the basis for numerous campaigns for equal pay and equal opportunities.

The Equal Pay Act and the Anti-Discrimination Act have managed to combine being one of the most significant achievements of the 1970s and one which affects most women's lives hardly at all:

> The focus of argument shifted: open disputes about whether or not women were men's inferiors, worthy of unequal treatment, gave way to disagreements over what exactly constituted the equal rights that women were acknowledged to deserve or how these could now be achieved. On the other hand, the material circumstance of most women's lives remained almost entirely unchanged by the new legislation. (Coote and Campbell, 1982, pp. 106–7.)

Nobody sat back after the implementation of the 1975 legislation and thought the battle was over. Legislation is always limited in what it can achieve, but the provision in Britain has proved to have many loopholes and opportunities for avoidance. A fundamental problem has been that it embodied an ideal of equality which rests on a comparison and measure with men. Where women do as men, they will be treated as men. Now apart from the fact that women do not want to become men, the strategies of employers in the five-year period before the implementation of equal pay sought ways to ensure that women were in jobs which would have no basis for comparison with men (Snell, 1979). Consequently, the implementation of equal pay probably *contributed* to increased job segregation on the basis of gender (Hakim, 1979, p. 49). By 1977, any possible improvements in women's pay to be achieved through the Equal Pay Act appeared to have reached their limits. Women's earnings stuck at 71 percent of men's (EOC, 1981c, p. 20), and now there is evidence that this relationship is actually deteriorating further (DOE, 1983).

Although men and women may now earn the same basic rates, men make up their earnings with shift premiums and bonuses, overtime pay, and payment for length of service and qualifications (EOC, 1981c, p. 20), whereas, on the whole, women do not earn those extra pay elements. Still, this is only part of the explanation for the ongoing differentiation of men's and women's pay. The fact of the matter is, that women do different jobs from men, cannot be directly compared with men, and women's work is persistently *undervalued*. The Equal Pay Act permits that to happen.

In 1982, the EEC court ruled that the Equal Pay Act in the United Kingdom was failing to comply with European law, because it did not provide for the principle of equal pay for work of equal value. The Equal Opportunities Commission has long sought the incorporation of this principle into the existing legislation because direct comparison with men becomes unnecessary, and it allows for a re-evaluation and upgrading of women's work. In response to the European Court, the Thatcher government is now seeking to pass a Bill in 1983, to comply with EEC regulations. Although the wording of the drafted Bill 'allows women to define their work as of equal importance to the work traditionally undertaken by men . . . it is highly unlikely that the law presently proposed can ever

139

have such effects. It is drafted in such a way as to make equal pay for work of equal value almost impossible to claim' (Atkins, 1983).

Positive Action

Partly in recognition of the limitations of legislation by itself, there has in the last few years been gathering support for a positive action programme for women. The idea is that women have much more than formal barriers to overcome, and that radical action and intervention is required to ensure that women do get their share of jobs, training, promotion and pay. Positive action for women is now reflected, to varying degrees, in training schemes, trade union organisation and local authority policies.

Training courses for women only are now being funded by the Manpower Services Commission and the European Social Funds. They provide women with training for skills and employment in areas which have not been readily open to women. In a similar vein, some local authorities have become equal opportunities employers, where the local authority, as employers, give direction on how to facilitate equal opportunities for women. Perhaps the most notable example of this local authority initiative has been the Greater London Council's programme which has set up a special women's unit. Other local authorities have similar programmes. It involves a major commitment to establishing equality of opportunity in recruitment, training and promotion, as well as providing the facilities, such as childcare provision and flexible working time, to make that *genuinely* possible. In setting up these programmes local authorities are providing a model of employment practice. Amongst employers in private industry there has been little take up of positive action policies, although it is there that. some of the most blatant barriers to women's opportunities exist.

The TUC has also given its official support to a positive action programme for equal opportunities. Now many trade unions have special women's committees, officials with responsibility for women, special education facilities for women, women's conferences and so on. The greatest changes have occurred in those unions with a large female membership, especially white collar, public service unions, where women trade unionists have pushed women's issues on to the agenda.

Flexible and Shorter Working Hours

Women still have most, if not all, of the responsibility for childcare and domestic labour. While this is the case, it is often very difficult for women to take up well-paid, more responsible jobs because the hours of work are too long, or too inflexible, to combine with family responsibilities. This barrier to equal opportunities could be overcome by more flexible, shorter working arrangements, which do not forfeit employment protection and rights in the way that part-time work does. The Equal Opportunities Commission has proposed various forms of alternative working arrangements: flexi-time, shorter working time and job sharing, and indicated how they could be implemented (EOC, 1981b), but such proposals have met with a lot of resistance from employers who argue that the organisation of more skilled work does not easily lend itself to flexible and shorter working arrangements.

The most radical proposal for such new working arrangements to meet the needs of women has been to seek the extension of full-time rights to part-time workers. The EEC has issued a draft directive to the governments of the European Community for such legislative provision to be in operation by 1983. This did not happen, and the directive was hotly resisted on grounds of impracticability and expense. The battle to implement such legislation will doubtless be similar to the protracted and prolonged implementation of the Equal Pay Act. Indeed arguments against the current proposals are very similar – that such employment protection will undermine the cost advantage of employing women and they will simply not be employed. Yet if women have no greater value than their vulnerability to increased exploitation, then in itself that is a reason for legislative redress.

Women's demands for shorter and more flexible working time have up until recently received cursory attention from employers, trade unions and government, but now in deepening recession and high levels of unemployment, they have relevance as a strategy for tackling unemployment and job shortage. In 1982, the Thatcher government introduced a scheme for work sharing, it was implemented in January 1983. Its introduction made a considerable departure from Tory policy which up until then had been resistant to any proposals for work sharing or shorter working time. It reflects how the government policies are contradictorily caught between concern for the social and political instability and high welfare costs, arising from high unemployment, on the one hand and the high utility value of unemployment in controlling labour and wage demands, on the other. The scheme for work sharing, or job splitting as it is called, provides a grant to employers to divide a job into two half jobs. So far only the most routine jobs are being considered for job splitting and recent advice from the Confederation of British Industry to its members indicates that if a split job is kept below 16 hours a week, then employers can avoid some liability under the Employment Protection Act. It remains to be seen how the scheme will develop, but there is every reason to fear that job splitting may be open to all the abuses of part-time work. It is a scheme aimed implicitly at unemployed youth, rather than the labour force in general. Many married women are automatically excluded since only those in receipt of Unemployment Benefit or Supplementary Benefit are eligible for jobs created by job splitting. It most certainly does not arise from any concern with equal opportunities for women.

Now many trade unions are also negotiating *reduced working hours* as part of a wage agreement. In 1975, the TUC formally adopted the European Trade Unions Confederation's programme for a reduction in working time. The TUC now holds an official policy of a 35-hour week, six weeks' holiday and early retirement options, as well as seeking restrictions on overtime working. There is after all nothing God-given about the 40-hour week. At the

142

beginning of the twentieth century full-time work meant 60 hours a week, over six days a week. The working week has progressively diminished and although the Thatcher government has not encouraged reduced working time, nevertheless, by 1981, five million workers in the UK were covered by reduced working hours' agreements (Industrial Relations Services, 1981, pp. 8–11). Trade union support for forms of work sharing: flexible working time, job sharing and full-time rights for part-timers, is less enthusiastic, although unions have had to respond to the growing demand for such facilities from their female members. There is still a fear amongst many trade unions that anything other than a full-time job amounts to job cutting and wage cutting. These fears arise in part from the trade unions' perception of part-timers as difficult to organise, but there is no reason why part-time jobs, with full protection and pro-rata payment, should menace full-time work. It is for the trade union movement to ensure that part-time workers have full representation within their trade unions.

Equal opportunities for women has been an ambiguous project. In principle its aims are far reaching, in practice they have been limited. Equality for women has been an integral part of the ideals of social democracy and links easily with its broader aims of equality, individual freedom and self-realisation. Yet women's equality has been 'purchased' by the economic expansion which created the jobs for women in the first place. The growth of women's employment has taken place within the parameters of capitalist production, capitalist relations and gender relations, which subordinate women to men. 'Equality' could be afforded in a period of economic and political well being, but was harnessed to it. No attempt was made to transform the basis of the relations of capital and labour, and of men and women. In recession the legacy of social democracy is a very fragile one.

The Problem with Men

In the last three decades, enormous changes have taken place in women's lives and yet it is possible to argue that fundamentally the

143

position of women remains unchanged. Women no longer expect their lives to be confined to the domain of childcare and domesticity, and now enter paid employment as a matter of normal circumstance, with formal equality with men. At the same time, women are more exploited than men at work, and at home women still have to assume the responsibility for housework and childcare. The two are linked. It has been possible to deepen the exploitation of women's labour whilst there exists a sexual division of labour which primarily defines women in terms of the family and the domestic. Equal opportunities have provided a programme for meeting, here and now, some of the most immediate needs of women. What is also needed is a programme which strikes at the very roots of gender divisions and women's subordination.

Employers will exploit existing divisions and weaknesses in order to cheapen their labour costs, unless they are prevented from doing so by either State legislation or working-class organisation. Women's employment is now more regulated by legislation than men's: the Factory Acts (1961), the Equal Pay Act and Anti-Discrimination Act (1975), combined with the Employment Protection Act (1980), now prevent the worst abuses of female labour. Yet at the same time, the State has only once in recent history cast its blessing on married women working and that was during the Second World War. Then women's entry into employment was facilitated by State nursery provision, canteens and flexible hours. Otherwise State legislation in the form of social welfare has always *reinforced* women as dependants in the family (Land, 1976; McIntosh, 1978), and has never had any commitment to accommodating women's working lives. Those measures which have in fact helped women to work, for example, school meals and some limited day-care provision, have always been perceived as measures for *child welfare*. Women have always had to manage *individually* and *privately* the tension between unpaid domestic work and paid employment.

The major reason why so many aspects of women's employment have had to be regulated by legislation, and State intervention, is because women have been less protected than men by working-class

organisation, the trade unions. The standard trade union perception of its female members has been that women are difficult to
organise and rather 'backward' in trade union affairs and, as
cheap labour, represent a threat to male wages. For men have long
opposed women's work where they have posed a threat to their
jobs, wages, manhood and privilege. Men have acted in ways
which have been oppositional to women's interests and have
reinforced their vulnerability to low pay (Boston, 1980; Lewenhak,
1977; Rowbotham, 1973). There have been some dramatic changes
in some trade union practices, especially in those unions which
have woken up to the fact that they have a predominantly female
membership. They have worked hard to increase female representation and are slowly realising that 'muscle' may no longer be the
most sophisticated trade union weapon. Nevertheless, it is still
very clear that trade unions organise primarily around the
interests of their male members, even where women form the
majority of the membership. Women's issues and struggles have
been neglected, marginalised and sometimes squashed. Men's
hostility towards women is never far away from the surface. They
have ignored women's struggles for equal pay (Snell, 1979), they
have suppressed women's industrial actions (Pollert, 1981) and
they continue to negotiate redundancy agreements in which
women are to go first (Vaughan, 1981).

There are a range of reasons why male trade unionists have
opposed women workers. Historically, women have often been
drawn into production as a direct threat to men's labour, but
men's strategies have not been to support women in their struggle
for equal pay, so that women could not be used to undercut the
male wage, rather they have sought to exclude them. All too often
men oppose women's interests, not because they represent a direct
threat but to maintain a system of inequality and privilege which
serves their short-term interests both at work and in the family.
There has been no commitment from male trade unionists to
recast domestic divisions. Men are the major recipients of
women's domestic labour *and* have deployed that domestic
arrangement to improve their relative position in waged labour.
Male forms of trade unionism have adopted collective bargaining

as their favoured form of wage offensive. It cannot serve the interests of women who are weakly organised, nor can it provide a *political* strategy for the working class:

> . . . free collective bargaining is not an effective socialist economic strategy against capitalism, nor is it in any way a strategy for women's equality. . . . The wages offensive can't be sustained as a political offensive against capital because it never actually confronts the problem of capital's *control* over the economy. . . . It is not a form of bargaining that includes all workers or is on behalf of all workers. It is a survival of the fittest strategy. (Campbell and Charlton, 1978, p. 34.)

Moreover, collective bargaining is based on a strategy for maintaining wage differentials, and thereby reinforcing them, and men have sought to maintain their higher pay by defining it in relation to women's lower pay. Men have persisted in their claim to earn more than women because they are the family breadwinners. The family wage is still the basis for male wage bargaining and as a piece of mythology is sustained, despite the fact that women's pay now makes up a major contribution to the income of most households. Most men are not sole family breadwinners but their claim to be undermines women's claim to equal pay.

Feminists have been very critical indeed of trade union practices, not from any desire to participate in right-wing 'union bashing', but from a concern that traditional forms of trade unionism, organised around the interests of men, leave women very vulnerable *and*, in the longer term, fail to provide a coherent *political* strategy: 'Trade unionism will be left loitering without interest in the pre-history of modern capitalism, a muscle-bound Tarzan, a man of few words wielding blunt instruments (Campbell, 1980, pp. 18-19).

Men's resistances to women have contributed to their own organisational weakness. Where male supremacy has been the life blood of working-class politics, this is especially so:

> Wales, like similar regions, may prove exceptional in the resistance it may offer to the demands of the working women's

movements. The very cultural formation of the historic Welsh working class may prove an unconscious accomplice in its renewed subjection. If the working class movement in Wales fails to respond, it will, like Wales itself, end up stranded on the margins of history, like some derelict whale on a polluted beach. (Williams, 1983.)

The trade union movement is in crisis. Its strength has been focused on the workplace and on the politics of expansion, and now for so many there is no workplace and no wage around which to bargain. It has primarily and historically been organised around the interests of the *male* working class, not the class as a whole, and its formerly strongest areas are now its weakest. The heavy industries which have been predominantly male industries, are now those most speedily in decline. Potentially, women could spearhead a new broader form of mass trade unionism and come to it without a history of, and sceptical of, short-term sectional gains. Women's relations to production and the family *forces* wider concerns and issues than the economic. Women place on the agenda not only income distribution, but also questions of working conditions, hours of work, consumption and childcare. Paradoxically, women's demands now have a wider relevance beyond 'women's issues' and could become central to a radical strategy against job shortage, poverty and inequality.

Worklessness could be tackled through a redistribution of work, *including* domestic labour and childcare in which men and women participate equally, by shorter working hours for everyone. Part-time work with full-time protection would cease to be a form of female ghettoisation, but an option for men too. The social wage, rather than pay, could be a focus for trade union organisation to overcome many of the divisions between those in work and those out of work, and between high-paid and low-paid workers.

Yet women's experiences of working-class politics *as women* raise crucial doubts about the possibilities of shared strategies and politics. Men have not only made life very difficult for women, but display in their class politics and organisation, an inherent conservatism. At the end of the day, can women rely on men? Men may now be seeking some redistribution of work, but that does not extend to any support of women's right to work, nor the right to a decent living wage, nor for any redistribution of domestic responsibility. The times require offensive strategies and politics of vision, but can men let go?

Notes

1. It is very probable that statistics have always and will continue to undercount the extent of married women's employment. Many married women work on the 'fringe' of the economy, working insufficient hours, or earning insufficient pay, to be incorporated in National Insurance coverage. Different data sources tend to come up with different figures (DoE, 1973).

2. The Trades Union Congress has estimated that if all the unregistered unemployed and those on short-term training schemes were to be included, then the figure would be nearing five million (TUC, 1982).

3. A standard performance is the output target that management set for each operator. It is measured in 1/100 units, so a 100 performance represents the management target. An operator who achieves a 50 performance has only produced half the amount of work set for her to do in a given time. An operator who has a 125 performance has on the other hand excelled herself, and her output is a quarter higher than that set by management.

4. One possible future development is for small firms to 'share' new cutting equipment.

5. Out of a total of 76 women whom I contacted after the redundancy, two had gone 'off market'; one because she was nearly 60 and the other because of pregnancy.

6. In October 1982, following the recommendations of the Rayner Report, some 160,000 people who had registered but were not entitled to benefit, are no longer able to do so. This includes self-employed men and many married women. It will be of some comfort that if they cannot register they cannot be unemployed either.

7. The Redundancy Payments Scheme is not intended to make unemployment easier, but to render labour less resistant to restructuring and job loss (Fryer, 1981). In the event of long-term unemployment it is inadequate compensation, but at the time of redundancy it can offer undreamed of sums of money. It is hard for both men and women not to be ambivalent about redundancy.

8. Indeed as regions, which were once the traditional site of the *male* working class, shed more and more men's jobs, so women's jobs flourish. It may be that particularly well-organised practices of exclusion made women a 'super cheap' labour reserve, and this is now reflected in the growth of women's jobs, *especially* in those regions (Wales, Scotland and the North East) which were once heavily associated with male employment (Massey, 1983).

References

Place of publication is London unless otherwise stated.

Alexander, S., 'Introduction', in M. Herzog, *From Hand to Mouth*, Penguin, 1980.

Atkins, S., 'New Hurdles for Women to Surmount in the Race for Equal Pay', *Guardian*, 28 March 1983.

Baran, P. and Sweezey, P., *Monopoly Capital*, Penguin, 1973.

Barker, J. and Downing, H,. 'Word Processing and the Transformation of Patriarchal Relations of Control in the Office', *Capital and Class*, No. 10, pp. 64–99, 1980.

Barrett, M., *Women's Oppression Today*, Verso, 1980.

Barron, D. and Norris, G. M., 'Sexual Divisions and the Dual Labour Market' in D. L. Barker and S. Allen (eds), *Dependence and Exploitation in Work and Marriage*, Longman, 1976.

Beechey, V., 'Some Notes on Female Wage Labour in Capitalist Production', *Capital and Class*, No. 3, pp. 45–66, 1978.

Bland, L., Brunsdon, C., Hobson, D. and Winship, J., 'Women "Inside and Outside" the Relations of Production', in Women's Study Group, Centre for Contemporary Cultural Studies, *Women Take Issue*, Hutchinson, 1978.

Board of Trade, *Working Party Reports*, HMSO, 1947.

Boston, S., *Women Workers and the Trade Unions*, Davis Poynter, 1980.

Braverman, H., *Labour and Monopoly Capital*, Monthly Review Press, New York, 1974.

Brueghal, I., 'Women as a Reserve Army of Labour: A Note on Recent British Experience', *Feminist Review*, No. 3, pp. 12–23, 1979.

Business Statistics Office, *Business Monitor: Census of Production*, HMSO, 1976.

Campbell, B., 'Lining Their Pockets', *Time Out*, 13–19 July 1979.

Campbell, B., 'United We Fall: Women and the Wage Struggle', *Red Rag*, August 1980.

Campbell, B. and Charlton V., 'Work to Rule: Wages and the Family', *Red Rag*, pp. 30–6, 1978.

Central Statistics Office, *Social Trends*, No. 11, CSO, HMSO, 1981.

Chaney, J., *Social Networks and Job Information: the Situation of Women Who Return to Work*, Equal Opportunities Commission, Manchester, 1981.

Clothing Economic Development Council, *Report*, National Economic Development Office, HMSO, 1967.

151

References

Cockburn, C., *Brothers*, Pluto Press, 1983.

Community Development Project, *The Costs of Industrial Change*, CDP, 1977.

Cooper, C. and Davidson, N., *High Pressure: Working Lives of Women Managers*, Fontana, 1982.

Coote, A. and Campbell, B., *Sweet Freedom*, Picador, 1982.

Counter Information Services, 'Crisis: Women Under Attack', *Anti-Report*, No. 15, CIS, 1976.

Counter Information Services, 'Women in the 80s', *Anti-Report*, No. 28, CIS, 1980.

Coyle, A., 'Sex and Skill in the Clothing Industry', in J. West (ed.), *Work, Women and the Labour Market*, Routledge & Kegan Paul, 1982.

Cragg, A. and Dawson, T., 'Quantitative Research among Homeworkers', *Department of Employment Research Paper*, No. 21, Department of Employment, 1981.

Daniel, W., and Stilgoe, E., 'Where are They Now? A Follow Up Study of the Unemployed', *Political and Economic Planning*, Vol XLIII, No. 572, October 1977.

Dennis, N., Henriques, F. and Slaughter, C., *Coal is Our Life*, Tavistock, 1979.

Department of Employment, *Gazette*, 81 (II), DoE 1973.

Department of Employment, *Gazette*, 82 (I), DoE, 1974.

Department of Employment, *Gazette*, 89 (4), DoE, 1981.

Department of Employment, 'Patterns of Pay: Early Results of the 1983 New Earnings Survey', *Employment Gazette*, Vol. 9, No. 10, pp. 444–6, October, 1983.

Elias, P. and Main, B., *Women's Working Lives: Evidence from the National Training Survey*, University of Warwick Institute for Employment Research, 1982.

Elson, D. and Pearson, R., 'Nimble Fingers Make Cheap Workers: An Analysis of Women's Employment in Third World Export Manufacturing', *Feminist Review*, No. 7, pp. 87–107, 1981.

Equal Opportunities Commission, *Research Bulletin*, No. 1, Winter, EOC, Manchester, 1979.

Equal Opportunities Commission, *Alternative Working Arrangements 1*, EOC, Manchester, 1981a.

Equal Opportunities Commission, *Sixth Annual Report*, EOC, Manchester, 1981b.

Equal Opportunities Commission, 'Women and Underachievement at Work', *Research Bulletin*, No. 5, Spring, EOC, Manchester, 1981c.

Finn, D., Grant, N. and Johnson, R., 'Social Democracy, Education and the Crisis', in Centre for Contemporary Cultural Studies, *On Ideology, Working Papers in Cultural Studies*, CCCS, University of Birmingham, 1977.

Freeman, C., 'The "Understanding" Employer', in J. West (ed.), *Work, Women and the Labour Market*, Routledge & Kegan Paul, 1982.

Froebal, F., Heinrichs, J. and Kreye, O., *The New International Division of Labour*, Cambridge University Press, Cambridge, 1979.

Fryer, R., 'State, Redundancy and the Law', in R. Fryer, A. Hunt, D. McBarnett and B. Moorhouse (eds), *Law, State and Society*, Croom Helm, 1981.

Grossman, R., 'Women's Place in the Integrated Circuit', *South East Asia Chronicle*, No. 66, pp. 2–17 (joint issue with Pacific Research, Vol. 9, No. 5–6), 1979.

Hakim, C., 'Occupational Segregation', *Department of Employment Research Paper*, No. 9, November, Department of Employment, 1979.

Haringey and Lewisham Women's Employment Project, *Women, Where are Your Jobs Going?*, Haringey and Lewisham Women's Employment Project, 1981.

Hines, C. and Searle, G., *Automatic Unemployment*, Earth Resources Research, 1979.

Hird, C., Herman, G. and Taylor, R., 'The Textile Crisis', *New Statesman*, Vol. 100, No. 2585, October, pp. 12–14, 1980.

Hoel, B., 'Contemporary Clothing "Sweatshops", Asian Female Labour and Collective Organisation', in J. West (ed.), *Work, Women and the Labour Market*, Routledge & Kegan Paul, 1982.

Hope, E., Kennedy, M. and De Winter, A., 'Homeworkers in North London', in D. Leonard Barker and S. Allen (eds), *Dependence and Exploitation in Work and Marriage*, Longman, 1976.

House of Lords, *Voluntary Part-time Work*, Select Committee on the European Communities, Draft Directive 4053/82, HMSO, 1982.

Humphries, J., 'Women: Scapegoats and Safety Valves in the Great Depression', *Review of Radical Political Economies*, Vol. 8, No. 1, pp. 98–121, 1976.

Hurstfield, J., 'Part–Time Pittance', *Low Pay Review*, No. 7, pp. 1–15, 1980.

Hurstfield, J., *The Part–Time Trap*, Low Pay Unit, 1978.

Huws, U., *The Impact of New Technology on the Working Lives of Women in West Yorkshire*, Interim Report, Leeds Trade Union and Community Resource and Information Centre, 1980.

Huws, U., *Your Job in the Eighties*, Pluto Press, 1980.

Industrial Relations Services, *Industrial Relations Review and Report*, No. 257, pp. 8–11, 1981.

Institute for Employment Research, *Review of the Economy and Employment*, Spring, Institute for Employment Research, University of Warwick, 1982.

Jephcott, P., Seear, N. and Smith, J., *Married Women Working*, Allen & Unwin, 1962.

Land, H., 'Women: Supporters or Supported?', in D. Leonard Barker and S. Allen (eds), *Sexual Divisions and Society: Process and Change*, Tavistock, 1976.

Lewenhak, S., *Women and Trade Unions*, Ernest Benn, 1977.

Liff, S., 'Part–time Employment Among Women Factory Workers', *Employee Relations*, Vol. 3, No. 1, pp. 17–21, 1981.

Mandel, E., *Late Capitalism*, Verso, 1978.

Market Opinion Research International (MORI), in Peter Kellner, 'Maggie's Missing Million', *New Statesman*, Vol. 101 No. 2610, pp. 4–5, 1981.

Massey, D., 'The Shape of Things to Come', *Marxism Today*, Vol. 27, No. 4, April, pp. 18–27, 1983.

McIntosh, M., 'The State and the Oppression of Women', in A. Kuhn and A. M. Wolpe (eds), *Feminism and Materialism*, Routledge & Kegan Paul, 1978.

McRobbie, A., 'Working–class Girls and the Culture of Femininity', in Women's Studies Group, Centre for Contemporary Cultural Studies, *Women Take Issue*, Hutchinson, 1978.

Myrdal, A. and Klein, V., *Women's Two Roles*, Routledge & Kegan Paul, 1956.

Pollert, A., *Girls, Wives, Factory Lives*, Macmillan, 1981.

Purcell, K., 'Militancy and Acquiesence Amongst Women Workers', in S. Burman (ed.), *Fit Work for Women*, Croom Helm, 1979.

References

Rapoport, R. and Rapoport, R., *Dual Career Families*, Penguin, 1971.

Robinson, O., 'Part-time Labour: terms and conditions of employment', Paper presented to Joint Equal Opportunities Commission/Social Science Research Council Research Panel Conference on Part-Time Work, City University, London, 28 October 1982.

Roche, J., 'The Leeds Clothing Strike', in K. Coates, T. Topham, and M. Barrett-Brown (eds), *Trade Union Register*, No. 1, The Merlin Press, pp. 162–72, 1970.

Rowbotham, S., *Women's Consciousness, Man's World*, Penguin, 1973.

Royal Commission on the Distribution of Income and Wealth, *Lower Incomes*, Report No. 6, Cmnd. 7175, HMSO, 1978.

Rubery, J., 'Structured Labour Markets, Worker Organisation and Low Pay', *Cambridge Journal of Economics*, Vol. 2, No. 1, pp. 17–36, 1978.

Rubery, J. and Tarling, R., 'Women in Recession', paper presented to Socialist Economic Review Conference, September, 1981.

Ryan, M., 'Lee Jeans', *New Socialist*, No. 2, Nov.–Dec., pp. 24–5, 1981.

Sinfield, A., *What Unemployment Means*, Martin Robertson, Oxford, 1981.

Snell, M., 'The Equal Pay and Sex Discrimination Acts: Their Impact in the Workplace', *Feminist Review*, No. 1, pp. 37–58, 1979.

Study Commission on the Family, *Families in the Future*, Study Commission on the Family, 1983.

Tolson, A., *The Limits of Masculinity*, Tavistock, 1977.

Trades Union Congress, *Economic Research*, November, TUC, 1982.

Trade Union Community Resource and Information Centre, *TUCRIC Bulletin*, Aug.–Sept., No. 15, Leeds TUCRIC, 1980.

Vaughan, J., 'Ladies Who Won't Go First', *New Statesman*, Vol. 102, No. 2647, 11 December 1981.

Weir, A. and McIntosh, M., 'Towards a Wages Strategy for Women', *Feminist Review*, No. 10, pp. 5–20, 1982.

Williams, G., 'Land of Our Fathers', *Marxism Today*, Vol. 26, No. 8, August, pp. 22–30, 1982.

Williams, G., *Guardian*, 5 February 1983.

Williams, N., 'The New Sweat Shops', *New Society*, Vol. 20, No. 509, June, pp. 666–8, 1972.

Wood, S., 'Redundancy and Female Employment', *Sociological Review*, Vol. 29, No. 4, November, pp. 649–83, 1981.

Zweig, F., *Women's Life and Labour*, Victor Gollancz, 1952.